Foreword.

On 18th September 2014, Scotland was on the brink of Independence. Tensions, as well as hopes, were high in the Yes Campaign but the thought of a country unwilling to take control of its own destiny, being "happy" the way they were, were the overpowering factors set deep in everyone's mind as we went to the polls.

Yes Campaigns held pro-Independence rallies all over Scotland and were praised the world over for their commitment, and political knowledge, to their cause. Whilst Yes were taking their case to every doorstep in the country, the No Campaign with the British Government's backing were seen rarely in comparison. Scotland voted No but the lies and dirty tactics along with the intervention of Gordon Brown, promising a blank Vow, and ably backed by the biased media – in particular, Scotland's own Daily Record who printed this so called Vow signed by the 3 Amigos. David Cameron, Nick Clegg and Ed Miliband appeared as signatories the very next morning on the Daily Record's front page to a Vow which consisted of nothing, dreamt up by a former Prime Minister, Gordon Brown.

This is what won the case for the Union, in my opinion, the case to stay united in this disunited kingdom plus all their lies about the NHS, the life expectancy of our oil resources plus, of course the pensions. At one point, Alasdair Darling said oil would run out on **St Patrick's Day 2014**. I kid you not and none of the media picked this up, surprise, surprise! Labour put the fear of God into our senior citizens by calling them at home and stating that they would lose their pensions if they voted Yes. They also told our Polish, and other, workers that there was a strong chance they would be deported in an independent Scotland. Their depths know no bounds. All lies.

Our then First Minister of Scotland, Alex Salmond, stepped down just after that black day to pursue his career and stood for the SNP in the constituency of Gordon, in the General Election. It wasn't just Mr Salmond who was heading in Westminster's direction as a SNP MP but 56 out of 59 candidates in Scotland would wing their way down to represent the party of Scotland. And all flying the flag for Scottish Independence. Fifty five backing up Angus Robertson, our leader in the House of Commons who so far has done a magnificent job but with the backing of this lot, including the youngest MP for hundreds of years, Mhairi Black, things will only improve. The Scottish people will demand things improve!

Nicola Sturgeon is from a similar school of thought as AS but has her own particular views on how Scotland should be run. She succeeded "Oor Alex" in taking over the mantle of First Minister of Scotland and also the first woman to hold that position. The fact Alex Salmond stepped down left the way clear for the Independence debate to carry on but as Nicola said, it is not up to her, the Scottish Government or any politician but the will of the people of Scotland. I wish the BBC and the rest of the media had taken that on board as every single time she's interviewed, they bring it up. Scotland has changed and it's not that it cannot go back, it will not go back, it must not go back. Scots have awakened from a deep sleep and have the fight and conviction of a determined people, much more determined than those who want us to stay. It is no coincidence that a lot of English wished there was a candidate from SNP to represent them down south. I was at a meeting last February in London SNP Branch when a guest member asked the question: Could I stand as the SNP candidate in Croydon? He couldn't but that shows just how far we have come. When people ask why we are fighting for Independence, my answer is: Why not? It is unthinkable in this day and age that a country cannot govern itself and hopefully one day soon, we can be that free nation.

These poems reflect the positive side of the ongoing Yes movement and the negative depths to which the machine that is Westminster will stoop to get their way. I have tried to present them here in date order. Because of their lies and deceit, many of the No Campaign now wish they had voted Yes. Some are happy and uplifting while others show my own personal feelings towards Westminster, its politicians and the biased media which is run by them and backs them up at every opportunity. This is a media who cannot report truthfully or competently on rallies which take place on their doorstep. A government controlled media who ignore when 100,000 people march against Austerity in the centre of London. Their BBC told us that a few hundred attended the Hope Over Fear Rally in Glasgow early 2015 when the police and other media sources said there were 12,000. A coalition Government who along with Labour jumped into the king sized bed of political madness and are now indistinguishable from each other. Labour, for their part are dead in Scotland. Are they one and the same? It's reasonable to think so but one thing is for certain, we are not going away, we are not going anywhere. We are here for Independence, no matter how long it takes. I have had the privilege of meeting many of you this year and it was absolutely fantastic to finally see those people who have backed me from day one and encouraged my writings. For that I will be eternally grateful and I look forward to seeing those I have not yet met but to whom I owe so much.

When my first book, Poems For An Independent Scotland, was released, I was not able to thank the illustrator properly as I did not know her full name. I only knew her as Nicole. I would now like to take this opportunity to thank Nicole Summers for the stunning artwork she created with only a few ideas in mind of what I wanted. It is absolutely beautiful, a fantastic work for which I will be forever grateful. I still get a buzz when I see it. Thank you so much Nicole xx

Lastly, I was over the moon when wee Skribbles, aka Michael Larkin, agreed to do the artwork for this book. Thousands of you know him through his placards at rallies across the country, his bold and forthright posts on Facebook and many of you will have had your selfies with him. He truly is a gentleman. It is an honour for me to work with him and his beautiful fiancé, Fiona, will be Mr & Mrs Larkin this time next year. I am sure you will join me in wishing them all the very best in their lives together. XX

This is not the end.

Who better to open up with than Alex Salmond, former First Minister of Scotland and to whom so many, not just Scots, owe so much.

My Bonnet and Me.

(Sorry Alex for stealing a couple of your lines)!

I'm coming for battle and will charge at the gun

In order to right all the wrongs you have done

And indeed question motives as to why they're so wrong

And leave, if I must, from the land I belong.

I'm not some Pretender and for this seat I will vie

Yet some in Westminster have dared to ask why,

Why do you think? Can't you work this one out?

Well once I have spoken, you'll be left in no doubt!

Make ready your defence, I am fully prepared,

I'll let Westminster's bullies hear Scottish views aired

There will be no treason nor gunpowder plot

But I'll be fighting for Scotland and every damned Scot!

You broke every promise your government made

And now that I'm coming, be very afraid

So if I win Gordon's seat, please God let it be,

Then you'll see once again my dear bonnet and me.

Is It Just My Imagination?

Worldwide, the stories roll, straight off the steaming press

The headlines, death, destruction, our world is in distress

Shootings, murders, gangland rape, epidemics plague our
land

Terrorism rules the media and it's all out of our hands.

Wall Street, London, crash to banks so we pay the bankers' price

And along with politicians, they reap the richest prize

Between them, they've got it made, but who's controlling who?

It's a game of Happy Families in this monetary coup.

Way above the working man, the hierarchy rest

Playing chess with bombs and bullets with their pawns in battle dress

Wars are never near to home but they're never far away

And it's those who we elect to power, who have the final say

As to who will be our enemies and who will be our friends

As to where the battlefield will be, how and where these wars will end

Of what a nation's fate will be and how much each fight will cost

It's all about the money, not the million lives they lost.

Bomb the pawns by thousands, as planes fly overhead

Don't worry, they're civilians, the poor are better dead

Obliterating every street, and yes, more wars will come

And by the time they stop their war, they've made a princely sum.

The costs of bombs and bullets, is such a healthy trade

They rub their greedy hands with glee at the money they've just made

This lawless force bears all the costs that reshape these terrains

But as they own the factories: Replacements equals gains!

They manufacture everything for their fabricated wars

And revel in the ugly scenes that most of us abhor

Then they'll groom a future leader then render him a foe

A tyrant or dictator, he's sent where oil flows.

They start their wars through fear and claim they're being attacked

And the good old UK stands upright to guard America's back

They've bases here, there, everywhere and all are fully manned

They fight to make the rich more rich with death their final stand.

You're a hero if you're fighting, playing a patriot's game

But if you are a pacifist, you're a coward and will be shamed

We follow like the sheep we are as the wolves spin out their lies

But as each death brings a fortune, they care not who lives or dies.

How Many More?

Their methods and the men themselves should all be brought to hand

And would the courts deny us this in any other land

The feeble judge, spurred by the coin or to profit by their games

Where children play the starring roles but never know their names.

And who would back these "sinsisters" who bear the reaper's scythe

Their faces clothed in darkness, prey on the kids so blithe.

And the preacher from his pulpit, preaches sermons dark and stern

These holy beasts with solemn vows show no signs of concern

As they consecrate the parents then desecrate their son

Their evil deeds mean nothing as they take them one by one.

The tangled web of trust they weaved was tied off with contempt

And the children, they reached out to, were they made exempt?

The grandeur that's Balmoral, in the north part of this land

Home to the Royals, dignitaries and the gentry oh so grand

Yes, high class prostitution initially seems like joy

But not when you're sixteen years old, you're no more than a boy.

It's not just Balmoral Castle but the big one's named as well

If true of Buckingham Palace, then that's the main road into Hell

Their deeds and maybe even inner thoughts, scraped a nerve so raw

That our mal-adjusted government have abstained them with new laws

You've created human monsters who're now riddled with your guilt

Was it them, was it me? Look at what you've built

And just who are your neighbours, do they also crave young boys

And girls, who are silenced now, I hope one day they'll find a voice!

To investigate all paedophiles, they say the cost would be too great

Fifty thousand, that we know of, they'll let god decide their fate.

Happy Days!

Did you get all that you wanted? They made it sound so good

All those controversial powers they proposed to Holyrood

But just look what they gave you! Aye! Look at what you got

They care for Scotland's riches but they care not for the Scots.

We'll be getting extra powers but they've still to tell us what

They're even less than we rejected but maybe they forgot!

It's something we can build on and we'll get more in time

But meantime they're just doing us in with more political crimes.

Who is Lord Smith of Kelvin and where has this man been?

He's a smile with a suit on and his brief to me's obscene

He's only there for his pay-off just part of a greater act

And the fortune that awaits him? YOUR land's getting fracked!

On tax, at a meeting, they said we'd control Corporate Rates

Then "should" changed to "could" so again we must wait

They decided against it, yet again we're denied

Discussed then dismissed with no papers supplied.

No powers for jobs so that Scots can create

A workforce that's worthy and not let their fate

Be decided by Bullingdon, Westminster's boy band

Where some laws kill our people and others, our land.

Will the block grant be adjusted against what we raise?

There's not much to applaud and no-one to praise

But to burn Smith's Commission, was not only daft

Did they not realise it was only the draft!

There are things to be worked on but we gave up our rights

We'll get what they give us, we gave them that right

And their sanctions will prosper with Iain Duncan Smith

Did they throw out his court hearing or was that just a myth.

We are Their Hopes.

While the embarrassed shuffle aimlessly can we think what's in their head

What thoughts are they thinking, what words will be said?

The tears roll down your neighbour's face, what in life remains?

Tears from love or tears from joy can't match these hunger pains.

His tears are for the children, the embarrassment's his own

A pride he never doubted, questioned: has left him all alone

To him no pointless exercise, these questions must be asked

But the answers just elude him but he needs these answers fast.

"Why me, why us, why must I beg, I've done nothing wrong

I'm weak from hunger, I'm in pain yet tell myself I'm strong".

He's wandering his pointless life, a life that's crushing dreams

A voice that yesterday was soft is now only heard in screams.

He hides the tears and muffles cries as his children ask for food

Praying to his lord above, the god of all that's good.

Hopeless words are all he hears, and it's no use to complain

As the gentleman he speaks to, says, he's sanctioned once again.

Indignant manners, heartless rules, he hangs with baited breath

But the rules are made to end it all and based on certain death.

He can't accept acceptance, his pride is killing him

He's drowning in an austere flood and it's now too deep to swim

No words of hope can help him, he has hungry mouths to feed

But the cruel staff who paved his path are sowing deathly seeds.

Destruction is a mindset from the ruling upper class

And they'll carry on destroying, they're aiming for en-masse

Bit by bit they take away, what we'd call human rights

Dissolving any attitudes, anaesthetising fights

Poisoning our waters and poisoning our minds

All part of Westminster's designs on decline.

Actors All.

Gideon is Robin Hood, but he robs the poor to pay the rich

Then cuts a line of Charlie and phones for another bitch

Farage plays Lee Marvin, holding up some west end bar

Swilling beer, and hoping he's, that famous Wanderin' Star

Gordon Brown's a Dick -ens fan, playing Ebenezer Scrooge

In a jaw-dropping performance of a miser who's a stooge

Jackie Baillie's Madam Butterfly as she floats around the stage

Another mis-cast character, who's always on a different page

Leon Brittan is Hugh Hefner and commands we hear his voice

But instead of leading ladies, his escorts are all boys

Carmen's played by Theresa May and she's got Balls on tow

But Esther's at The Moulin Rouge in her own wee special show

The Angel With The Dirty Face has Nick Clegg in Cagney's role

The criminal who has changed of late but too late to save his soul

IDS is Hannibal, the man who silenced all our lambs

The ATOS Major General who hides behind his scams

Now wants us to stop breeding so our burden is removed

Such evil words from power and from a heart unmoved

Cameron is himself in this, he heads his elitist race

Warring with his people though his god would be disgraced

But he's doing such a brilliant job and hasn't fired a shot

His policies kill thousands, we're not worth a thought!

Another No Show.

Some need to get their stories told

Some are brave and some are bold

But they made sure each one was sold

He's worth his weight in gold!

This man, he has no dignity

And one who hates the SNP

The man who studied nine years free

And walked away with no degree!

By nature he will tell you lies

And that his precious Labour will not die

The man with blue and yellow ties

With him there is no compromise.

But if there's a vote he will not show

Then politely tell you where to go

He only goes where money grows

His name is one you know!

Katy Hopkins.

I remember Katy Hopkins, a lonely colleague on her own

Even then, yes, all those years ago, in a crowd she stood alone

She craved the world should love her but as now she was repelled

So she turned to me for friendship but this witch hailed from Hell.

I'm an easy touch for friendship but her ego was too great

One by one she asked for trust but in return she offered hate

A hatred that carries on today with her vile racist views

Re-tweeted by her followers to capture headline news

Shunned rightly by her colleagues then sacked by ITV

There's no place left for Katy, except the honourable BBC.

Her mind is filled with hatred but she's the problem not the cause

No wonder her nose is now a dick and from her chin hangs two big baws

It's quite an apt description for a friendless arrogant bitch

Who vilifies her country's poor because she's so bloody rich

But she's still that poor, this lost wee soul, that attention seeking girl

Who still craves love, affection, and who still blames this cruel world

It's never you, it never was, there was always someone else to blame

And your ego always emphasised how much you needed fame

You are one vindictive person, who may yet be arrested

And the only thing she'll take from life is how much she was detested.

Street Children.

Cold like stone, open, bare

Their naked eyes feel winter's stare

A child's thoughts, hopes and prayers

His Christmas gift, no-one was there!

All alone in their living fear,

No help will come by shedding tears

For no government will help out here

What hopes have children this New Year?

No roof, no home, their home's some street

And know in life they must compete

They vie for coins thrown at feet

While stores throw out their surplus meat

And yet the poor are still despised

But this nation's public's ill-advised

For the news we hear is all revised

But the truth is there before your eyes.

Can they expect life changing times

As the clock of life beneath them chimes

For harsh regimes are in their prime

And with them come these evil crimes

Yet the power lies within their hands

But to help these souls it seems is banned

Child poverty's here by their command

Upon every nation in these lands.

The Branch Secretary Has Spoken.

For the past forty years I backed you to the hilt

But you're no longer the Labour that Keir Hardie built

You care not for colours, blues, yellows or reds

And care not for the people as you messed with their heads

But you'd side with any who could further your cause

And once you were in, you dug in with your claws.

For forty years I've nurtured you but mis-trust has sealed your fate

You've gone from one I voted for to one I've grown to hate

I've been battered, bruised, punched and kicked through all of Labour's lies

But Scotland's standing firm now with an army on the rise.

We'll fight the Vow Brown promised which is now three years away

And the Scottish vote will see you gone, FOREVER, come this May!

Even now you've joined your greatest foe to oust The SNP

And already ousted one to date in a local council seat

But still you want the Tories out; Who is kidding who?

The internet's informing us and you haven't got a clue!

Do you think that we're all stupid, do you think we have no brains

Keep on doing what you do and then look at what remains!

Wee Duggie and Ms Dugdale, your colleagues and cohorts

Fill us with angry laughter with their precious tweets, retorts

You've lost the place completely with no policies your own

Except for funding all these nurses which your own party won't condone,

Unscrupulous and vindictive, it seems you've jumped the gun

Boris says you're mugging Londoners and it's only just begun

Yet part of the UK benefits is to pull and share resources

But it seems to me that Murphy's Law is aligned with darker forces

Do you really think they'll use the mansion tax to pay for just one nurse

I understand your logic but that's Westminster's purse!

Please tell us what you mean to do, we want to know your plan

You cannot promise anything but I'm sure you'll say you can.

Welcome To The Asylum.

We're not crazy but passionate, we're in between that finest line

That separates the meaningful from a quite distorted mind

We are run as an asylum so don't tell me that we're free

The madmen are our governments, their subjects, you and me!

They tell us how to spray our crops and spike our drinking water

The MSGs, the fluoride, forced on us, our sons and daughters,

McDonald's turn their dog food into something we can eat

By a spray of, yes, ammonia and have the cheek to call it meat.

Did we hear about Jamie Oliver when he took this lot to court?

No, the media, they were silenced and said, there's nothing to report!

Now they want to kill the earth itself, by fracking all our lands

All in the name of corporate money with governments' shake of hands.

Then as the queen looks through her honours list, she knows what's going on

It's a list of sex offenders yet not one name has been withdrawn

In fact she's said, she'll entertain, a convicted paedophile

Epstein, Prince Edward's paedophilic friend, will be her guest awhile

But it's no secret, paedophilia, runs deep in Royal veins

And whilst history has told us this, they don't like to mention weans

But this country can't accept that, we just do not comprehend

Why a prince befriends a paedophile but perhaps they're best of friends?

Savile, amongst others, was their guest in hielan' hames

Castles full of dark intrigue but under wraps were all the names

The silence here is deafening so what are they trying to hide

Or is it just a secret gathering, where fellow members self-confide?

Why does The Daily Telegraph condone this? These are evil, barbarous acts

And some politicians agree with this, do they scrub each others backs?

To say there's nothing wrong with this is disgusting, evil, vile

Are they themselves the crawling pimps or are they the paedophiles?

Question after question in this asylum's school of life

The answers lie with power lords, where corruption's always rife!

Their Golden god.

Even in the darkest moments, somewhere, someone sees the light

And the torch of this enlightenment is our daylight in their night

The more they hide, the more we seek, the more that we find out

The common man's a fearless foe, of that there is no doubt.

We're unravelling their spider's web and untangling their deceit

These conspirators who avert our words are the ones who feel the heat

Like the phoenix we have risen amidst their fanning flames

We're the wings of all that we survey and rejecting all false claims

For every lie they aim at us will cost them one more seat

We're soaring in the wind of change as they sink to their defeat

We hear lies contradicting lies as their aim is to subvert

A people who had once believed but we're a people now alert

We challenge every sentence, word and dissect every phrase

Yet these self-proclaimed almighties still howl their righteous praise

How good and great their party is and further they chastise

And preach of fire, brimstone, death, like some preacher on a high

They feed the rich and starve the poor and leave the sick to meet their hearse

How evil their Satanic quest, they quote the bible in reverse

Gold is the only god they worship, the one they honour and obey

Ensuring every war and law gives a rich rewarding day.

From The Bolsheviks to Royalty.

Mr Putin's revolutionaries are at it once again

For a submarine's been spotted, and it's Russian, near Faslane

The MOD has called for help, infiltrating us with Yanks

We've no naval vessels of our own so we'd just be firing blanks!

Our nuclear weapons, lying there, undefended and unused,

This deterrent shows us more than most how our money is abused

They say they're stopping others bombing us by just being on display

But the Ruskies can sail right down The Clyde and blow us all away!

What about security, can we afford to pay for staff?

The world is looking in on us with one big giant laugh

Banks are robbed here every day but nobody goes to court or jail

For the robbers are our men in suits who never cease to fail.

A world leader nowadays? A belief that's living in the past

And just in case you think we are, that is folly unsurpassed

You can't control Securicor, yet you can guard nuclear arms

No wonder Scotland's screaming out, for these to be disarmed!

We've got 50,000 citizens who've committed crimes against our kids

But that's far too many to accuse so the government shuts the lid,

Whilst one of these just wanders off to his ski-lodge to repair

And spends up to thirteen million pounds without a bloody care.

But why is Andy in the frame, has he upset his mum, the queen

Maybe she's just had enough with all The Royal's sex machines

I thought their deeds were under wraps, all so secretive, hush-hush

But every time we think we've won, they play their Royal Flush!

They don't do embarrassment, our Royals don't do faces red

Not even when the under-age, allegedly, in their beds

I know that he's not guilty, yet, but he's kept right out the way

I fear the Royals know much more than they're inclined to say

But remember who their cousins are, Gideon and big Dave!

That's two reasons for this secrecy and why all their crimes are waived!

Shark Infested Waters.

To think logically and outside their box is to conspire, even scheme

To question's unacceptable, a damning of this great machine

To undermine their sterling work is against their power regime

But the well oiled system, finely tuned, is not all as it seems.

Infiltration is their middle name, control's their first and last

Falsifying every speech, their lying's unsurpassed

Clinging to a commonwealth that lies buried in the past

But they've a chamber fit for royals where the sleeping Lords amass.

They have evil in their make-up, destruction in their mind

Unguarded nuclear missiles to keep their pockets lined

Unprovoked, unnerving wars are forced upon the blind

And the very ones who vote them in are cruelly undermined.

We're brainwashed with blinkered eyes, we let big brother take control

In their shark infested waters we're just minnows in their bowl

But suppressed we cannot carry on, only victory consoles

And the people here can have that when they vote in this year's polls.

Invisibility.

Education is their enemy, pure knowledge is their foe

We're armed with healthy options they don't want us to know

We're informed, educated, by the social media they designed

And now our heritage and culture will soon be redefined.

In the past submissive selves gave in and showed the controllers adulation

But the pain of unheard voices, still cry out for salvation

We were never in the dialogue; we're always outside looking in

As invisible voices answered us but kept their secrets deep within.

A contactless society where answers can't and don't exist

Wrapped loosely around pleasantries, they float off in the mist

I hear them sneer at words in prose, criticising what they preach

In the hope that we'll submit once more but now we're out of reach.

We are not those self-defeatists who entrench themselves with fear

But we've hearts that won't stop beating for the country we revere

And succumb no more to policies that determine and abuse

This country's vulnerable citizens, the disabled, old, confused

From a gang of legal crime lords who deem themselves invincible

Just fun loving criminals who, to us, remain invisible.

Great Scots!

We've riches beyond your wildest dreams

Though poor, we Scots are treasured

We're small with huge ambitions

With every outline measured

These borderlines have histories

From a rich and varied past

And the list of famous Scots below

Are no less than world class...........

Aboard The Flying Scotsman, I dined with one, James Watt

And while Pinkerton sought outlaws I read Sir Walter Scott

Then cycled on MacMillan's bike with tyres from Dunlop

On roads built by Tar Macadam 'til I found a camera shop

I saw Maxwell's colour photographs beside a fax from Ally Bain

Then watched TV with Logie Baird an' a' Jock Thampson's bairns

Watson-Watt served up some food from his new found microwave

While Fleming's penicillin saved us from early graves

I stood with Bruce at Bannockburn and fought in World War Two

Then joined the Tartan Army to march with Wallace too

I heard Rabbie Burns talk to a mouse whilst scribbling some words down

Then waved to passing Clyde-built ships, sailing from John Brown's

The Discovery rests by Dundee's quay so elegant at night

Lit by, James Bowman Lindsay, who gave the world electric lights

I took a rest on Telford's bridge and thought of Adam Smith

Who gave the world their economics and fought injustices we live with

Lister, Bell, Dewar, Black, like so many other Scots

Have enriched the world we live in with their Scottish school of thought

Traditions hold and cultures stay with a pride that covets each new day

And I leave with Burns' famous words, I bid you, Scots Wha Hae.

Fat Cats and Fat People.

Blame the poor, the immigrants, now it's blame the bloody fat

For scrounging off society when it's so much more than that

There are many shapes and sizes who are an asset and a boon

And there are those who're born in poverty and then those with silver spoons.

Laziness, I can't condone but there are those who try for jobs

But because there's no work out there, they're labelled as fat slobs

Idleness is everywhere, in every city, village, town,

And obesity's an illness which should not be frowned upon.

Yes we've those who overeat but we have this in reverse

We've bulimia, anorexia, are these not an equal curse?

But why do you ignore the bankers who got us in this mess?

Like magicians they issue credit notes straight out of nothingness

Where does this credit come from as it's plucked out of thin air

These golden cards, a Rothschild's dream, the man who says it's fair

Or the politicians, corporate Lords, who make sponging, seem routine

Or the Fat Cats who avoid their taxes, now that to me's obscene.

Is it fair to issue bonuses when our country's on its knees?

Yet these guys blame poor citizens for their austere disease

And as the debts grow deeper, they say they're in control

Spiralling through the corporate world into the same black hole

That black hole's that exists for them, always has and always will

Where corporations get their kicks and feed their corporate thrills

These people thrive on credit, on wars they say they hate

The same guys who pretend to love but in reality, seal our fate.

They tell us we are in their hearts and say they really care

But they'd rather be without us: That's how much they care!

They're our jailers in their great big house, we're the prisoners outside

Every five years changing jailers and it's us who do decide

But the stories just remain the same where they sing the same old song

And these austere acts they advocate is seen by us as wrong!

Don't Let Them Forget!

In a poem, Heather wrote a line: "What do poets do"?

'Til then I never thought of it but know I write for you

Your compliments and comments encouraged me to write

At first, the Referendum, where we thought we'd win outright

But instead of just laying down, we rose as a family of friends

We each made a silent promise, we'd fight this to the end.

From North to South and East to West, we met up every day

From leafleting to canvassing it was smiles all the way

With friendships formed you knew would last, it energised our souls

And the world looked to Scotland as we headed to the polls

Every day the sun would shine even in the sleet and snow

Meetings, hustings, rallying to, the place you had to go.

I never heard a murmur, no, not a single sound

Exhausted, sleepy, hungry, you turned the political world around

Reporting back when you got home, what happened on the night

Then off to bed and up at dawn to carry on the fight.

Smiling words fell, page on page, as you plotted your next meet

Or just knocked on the doors you saw in every single street

The laughter tore through pages and on Facebook every night

You were buzzing with this new found pride and set Scotland alight.

At work, in shops, that's all you heard: Are you voting Yes or No?

I miss those happy, smiling times, we lost but we all know

That those friendships weren't for nothing, we each gained a thousand friends

Some of whom we'll never meet but we'd trust them to the end

But when you meet a Facebook name, your heart jumps out your skin

And that precise excited moment is still with you deep within.

I was with you every step and feel what you all felt

Devastation and bewilderment as you tried to get them telt

They're part of that one special year and as friends they still remain

So plan your course and plot your moves; We're On The Road Again!

All those doors you knocked on, all the folks you met

Remind each one of all the lies, don't let them forget

Each one of you is special, backed by your special friends

So let's do this one together and buck these voting trends.

Westminster has to pay a price, they were shown to lie and cheat,

Tell that to all your neighbours and to all you meet and greet

And get The Yes signs up again with your Saltires flying high

And rid Scotland of red Tories, kiss all of them goodbye

Let Scotland's voice be rightly heard in London' house of power

And let them know democracy from voices that are ours

Oh I write with pride, I feel that pride, a pride that comes from you

And this proud hand will always write for you – That's what poets do. X

My Street's Now My Bed.

I'm rich, fuck off, and lie down in your street

Curl up in your blanket with that dog by your feet

Sleep through the wind, your rain, sleet or snow

With your fortune that's begged from folk you don't know

Cuddling up to your buddy in your nightly abyss

Does your dog bring you comfort as you lie in your piss?

My friend, don't be derogatory, there's no need to be rude

Your assumptions are wrong of this man whom you've viewed

My profession's in teaching but your governments' cuts

Have left me and more, in death or in ruts

I had a mortgage which I could not repay

My son and my daughter were both taken away

They put them in care and me on the streets

At least they've a roof and a bed with clean sheets

And now rightly or wrongly I tend for myself

And am fed not by you but from tins on a shelf

Provided not by you but by foodbanks in town

Supplied not by you but by the people around

Who have real social justice and their considered view

Is, they're willing to share unlike people like you

They have a conscience and help out when they can

As you hold the small fortune begged from folks you don't

And being human beings, help their fellow man

So please let me sleep and take your contempt

To the place it all started: Your damned government!

The Charismatic Secretary.

This Charismatic Secretary with the charismatic voice

Told us that he'd made a convert and left the Yes man with no choice

The next thing he's on Twitter telling us his latest scoop

He said the Yes man was converted but the truth is, he was duped.

It seems the Yes man joined his party for a measly, paltry pound

And the Charismatic Secretary had his tables turned right round,

This was vengeance for his lying and projecting all his fear

Now you can watch him and his party, drown for just a pound a year

Your Membership is rising but have you thought about the cost?

With your print and postage, salaries, you're running at a loss

And these pound a year new members will be filling all your halls

Shouting down all your proposals and heckling all your calls.

And of the Charismatic Secretary, they've seen neither hide nor hair

For the wily one is hiding out, in his foxy Glasgow lair

He's daft but he's not silly and tomorrow will be back,

I think the CS, big bad Jim, just enjoys the craic

For this Charismatic Secretary still can't seem to use his brain

But he'll soon be out of Scotland and back in London wi' his ain!

Silence The Lambs.

Some hearts come alive with the mention of gold

It lights up their face but inside they're still cold

And some, through no usage, are creeping with mould

For when greed takes the heart it can't be controlled.

When you ask them a question, they ask about cost

Their own wealth they measure by how much they have lost

Like sheep they would blether then follow their host

To a futile existence while they constantly boast.

Scotland once spoke out but now some succumb

To the houses of power who are banging their drum

But half are still shouting while the rest are struck dumb

Yet it's these who are shouting how great we've become!

And let the fires of September your hearts reignite

That excitement and passion to set Scotland alight

And show that we're ready and put those to flight

Who damned every rally but they knew we were right.

Indy Deb's and Bob Costello's Icy Adventure.

Murphy, the bold yin, headed up to Dundee

But ignored every person, he happened to see

He was there to convert all who voted Yes

But did he? You tell me! I'll give you one guess!

He saw then avoided each person he met

But Dundee is a city he'd rather forget.

Bombarded with questions yet no answers were found

The last time the egg man stepped on Yes City's ground

At least then he spoke but this time completely ignored

Our own Bob Costello with his giant YES board

And your own Iain Bryson alive on the pipes

While young Amy Black was there earning her stripes

And poor Indy Deb was left lagging behind

In the hope that one word, Dundee's air would grind.

She asked about sanctions and then suicide

So why didn't he answer, has he something to hide?

Well he answered one question in the cold silent air

He's a conman, a cheat, liar extraordinaire

We were hoping this time he'd have something to say

But he trudged through the snow and then drove away.

Again the Branch Secretary showed contempt and abuse

But I'm sure when he tweets, he'll say they were all full of booze!

Why broadcast a visit, why say you will meet

And convert all YES voters you'll meet in the street

What is your excuse for being so ignorant and rude

With actions like these you won't see Holyrood!

Would you drop us a line to say sorry to those

Who braved it to see you and nearly damn

You act like a numpty in the way you behave

You show no respect but expect us to save

A party that's littered with liars and cheats

With a leader who's heading to their worst ever defeat

Murphy lives in a world where life is a farce

Yer tea's oot ya coward, you talk through your arse!

The Streets of a City.

(Inspired by Frankie Miller's Drunken Nights).

I'll tell you a story of a man on his knees

Who figured he'd get me to see

His ways of deception, cheating and lies

As he laughed through cold steel blue eyes

We spoke about sanctions and people who'd died

And those who were sleeping outside

Then talked about bedrooms,

Its infamous tax

And weapons that stand on the Clyde.

He got to his feet and figured discreetly

What he thought I'd want to know

But I just shook my head

Stared at him and said

It's your own folk who've died in your show.

So he called to his maker

To pray for his soul

The best way he thought the best

Just another statistic

Who failed in the test

Yet another one laid down to rest.

That's our governing body

The government's way

The price we all have to pay

But come the election

The people will say

Labour will be gone come this May.

Another night in a city

Somewhere near you

Acquaintances lie on their streets

But as you close your front door

You cannot ignore

It was you they were hoping to meet.

Sleepless Nights.

Those sleepless nights you had back then

Are coming back again,

Haunting every heart and soul

From that bitter fought campaign,

Thoughts raced through a tortured mind

That left you feeling drained

But you'll never reminisce enough

'til you're drinking their champagne.

That apathy kept you awake

And how you cursed and swore

At the ones who wouldn't listen,

As you knocked upon their door

Every step you took was lightened

With a dance and happy song

You were forthright, determined

With beliefs that were so strong,

Approaching the homes of folks you knew

Of those you thought as friends

But as you asked them to back you

They could only pretend.

People cried proudly

In this beautiful land

It was a sight and a feeling

Some could not understand,

The majority voted

And you were undone

That battle was lost

Now there's a war to be won.

You're up against criminals

And up against minds

Who detest all you stand for

Who don't like your kind

A people who think

Who see way beyond

The treacherous deeds of

Political wands

Casting their spells

Distributing fear

Through a campaign of lies

The same as last year

When will they wake up

Those you thought friends

Today is a good time

Let's see how it ends.

The Brochure.

A colourful brochure was popped through my door

Aimed at progressing the plunge of the poor

The cost and its size saying what they've achieved

If it wasn't so grand maybe I would've believed,

How the job market's grown, the economy's great

How Britain's recovered from a doomed welfare state

How we're all better off we've more cash in our tails

And how Labour's to blame if they've made any fails

How we're turning the corner of times that were tough

And of the joyous expressions on those sleeping rough

They'll eradicate poverty, they'll cleanse city's streets

By spiking their beds they'll force a hasty retreat

And hope they'll take flats, treat them like city gents

And at three grand a month, it's no problem to rent.

Asking for voters to vote for these whores

And nothing on Trident it's not on these shores

Yet not one word was mentioned about our great NHS

It just goes to show they couldn't care less

But they care about us and they care about health

The only thing they want is more and more wealth

They'll sell to their mates or who bids the most

If they could they would sell to the great Holy Ghost

But they'll sell it to someone to just bloody well sell

They'll grab what they can and keep it themselves

There's not too much left that is publicly owned

I know that sounds harsh but King Dave's on the throne

Their assets are ours and they'll do as they're told

We'll make free speech redundant, get that on the news

They can say all they want but we won't accept views

We're masters of peasants and top of our trade

And, like others, won't admit to mistakes that we've made

Nobody does, they're all one and the same

Just a mixture of colours under three different names

And what about Ukip, enough has been said

They're just knitted from hate with no brains in their heads

Trying to corrupt all our friends who live in the south

By the bile they spew from an uncouth, evil mouth

But they're clearly just stupid and don't get the point

But if that's their agenda, they do not disappoint!

I don't mention Labour or the man with the crate

One who'll be missing come the great TV Debate

Because he's not a leader and I don't mean to sour

His bold reputation but he knows nothing of power

And can't use his brain, he's no common sense

He just steals opinions then sits on the fence.

And what of the brochure, will King David win?

Oh! That'll be the one, I just threw in the bin!

The Gambler.

Integrity questioned decisions we'd made

As the cards on the table were laid

Your sleeves hid the answers on this joker's parade

As you turned out the black queen of spades

You were just playing games with our hearts as the stakes

And the hearts makes many mistakes

You poisoned these hearts so you'd make the grade

And your queen made sure you were paid.

But the tables are turning; it's our turn to deal

And the stakes we play are for real

And your coveted seats will be tartan and sweet

Tell me, Labour, how does that feel?

You've ruled now in Glasgow for eighty long years

And still you pick on the poor

You cheated and lied to your own kith and kin

As you knocked, with a smile, on our door

You deserted a people, a nation, a race

As you welcomed your Tories to bed

Yet you still wear the red, of a party that's dead

But you're all wearing Cameron's head!

You can kill all the dreamers but the dream will live on

And you'll see it at every new dawn

You can't touch it or feel it but you know that it's there

It's only for people who care

But this time it's goodbye and our dream cannot die

For us, the stakes are too high.

His Wife's Role.

The wedding day and all is set as we hear the church bells chimes

And here she comes, the blushing bride, who'll hide a husband's crimes

The glowing skin, the flowing dress, the veil that hides a face

The virgin white she's wearing now will soon forever be disgraced.

They fill the church through circumstance, hypocrisy and gall

The highest orders in our land, Oh! How the mighty fall

Politicians, royalty, stars who are world renowned

Some self proclaimed, self righteous, the all pompous gather round.

But tell me little lady, tell me the thoughts you knew

Were you thrown into the Lion's Den, as so many more like you

You're living in denial, denying all you'd ever known

And all because of glamour and a little Barbie throne.

They taught you all their little rules and how the game was played

Then showered you with fineries and with jewels custom made

To stop a wife from crying and to stay down on on her knees

As he bedded child escorts: You knew he was diseased!

Did you miss his midnight kisses or those dances in the dark

And did you not think it very strange that his love had no spark?

You're as guilty as he ever was. You shut up for his cause

What you don't know, you can't admit so can't break his laws.

Why don't you just leave him and tell the world what you know?

You know the shameful sin you live as your screaming head shouts No!

You could say now, so tell me, tell me why you wait

For your heart grows ever colder in this life you've grown to hate.

THATCHER.

In death we go with nothing, leaving only memories behind

A few tokens, maybe photographs and treasures, of a kind

Would you cry for starving families, the destitute, the poor

No! But you shed tears for a woman who put them at death's door!

Some cried for you , we all know who, the queen of all austerity

The one who ruled with iron fist and a face full of sincerity

The legacy she left us all, is one that cannot heal

A memory for all of us, one we still see and feel,

It lingers in the air we breathe, in the hearts of grown men

Just the name of Margaret Thatcher gets the blood boiling again.

You won't see tears from these eyes, they witnessed what you done

We now see how corrupt she was now this woman's gone

Through exposing this corruption we find bankers, paedophiles

Stars who children idolised, were hidden by her smile.

What kind of god did you adore, worship or pray to

Was it the devil incarnate, reminding you of YOU?

You took a million families down and then went back for more

Some revered you as a saint, others say, the devil's spore!

Your regime against the working class, though buried in the past,

Will ensure the Thatcher name lives on, oh yes, your legacy will last.

At the forges and the steelworks, the furnaces don't burn

The cogs seized on machinery, their wheels no longer turn

The factory gates lie rusted, our waterways are still

The jobs are dead but more than that, it was the million hearts you killed,

Some are brought into this world to spread the word of peace

But you destroyed all in your path, consumed all like a beast

Now they're calling for a museum in honour of your name

Is it not enough your portrait hangs in the Tories Hall of Fame?

Your words were laced with cyanide and you done nothing but degrade

And primarily, it's thanks to you, we don't have British Made!

Post Referendum Bias.

Is it paranoia, bias or just me going off my head?

Why do I even listen to the crap of these inbreds?

The BBC show Nicola in a thirty second clip

Then let loose the lawmen shooting from the hip.

Her policies were shot to bits with no chance of recourse

So typical of this biased bunch, is this now Labour's tour de force?

It's the referendum's nightmare being shown all over again

It's obvious, no lesson's learned, the BBC's our bane.

The charismatic secretary, known as creepy Jim,

Seems to capture all the headlines, put in front of our FM

We read daily of her exploits and we hear of what she says

But is seldom seem responding thus causing our malaise

But they won't pitch her with her rivals, incase they're verbally torn to shreds

No, they avoid it like the plague and instead mess with our heads

They show arrogance by ignoring us and contempt to those who pay

The salaries of the arrogant but we will have our day!

The Man.

Just a keepsake from the memories that still live in our minds

Just a memory to cherish for the sake of Auld Lang Syne

Of a man who we all got to know, our country's number one,

We may have lost the battle but there's a war there to be won.

He gave us hope, he banished fear and told us to stand strong

He asked us to look to our hearts and nothing could go wrong

He could have been a Labour man, a peer by royal decree

But he chose to fight for Scottish hearts and joined The SNP.

Through the ranks he pushed his way and was banned from London's halls

For showing he had mettle and a man who had the balls

No stranger to controversy, he told you what he thought

And the mealy mouthed who challenged him, deserved all that they got.

Feared by politicians, adored by those he'd meet

He found no shame in passing time with those put on the streets

Taking time for passers-by and those out on a limb

A blether, smile, a laugh or two, his ain folk were for him.

But the laughter turned to Scottish roars when he fought for Scotland's rights

He took them on and let them know that they'd been in a fight

He led us once, is with us now, and standing by our side

He stands with you on every street and takes your every stride.

He's just a man but what a man, Scotland is his heart

But the referendum's come and gone, today is our new start

Now Gordon's known worldwide such is the great man's fame

And if you haven't guessed by now, Alex Salmond is his name

He's drawing up his final plans so we can have a say

And he knows that we are with him, with him all the way

We've had the fear and heard the lies and felt the real force of deceit

So now's the time to get the SNP those precious Westminster seats.

We owe him as we owe ourselves and owe Scotland one last chance

And then you'll see Oor Twinkle Toes, show Westminster how to dance!

Drink, The Curse of Labour?

It's the top of his agenda, the priority on his list

To make this a better country, this man's mouth is one big cyst,

For he wants to bring back alcohol, yes, you heard that right

At football grounds throughout this land, to fuel more fans' fights!

His reckless mouth's been opened our ears feel the pain

Our minds are now in overdrive because drinking is our bane

For all I see is vandalism, violence, chaos, panic, fear,

And maybe even death itself and no-one wants that here

Add to that the cost of policing, if Clubs could afford the cost

And with the families that stayed away, they'd be starting at a loss

Add destruction to our transport with mobs rioting on our streets

Then contemplate our hospitals and the deadlines they've to meet

And a match with fewer fans around doesn't bode well for our game

And if this is what Jim Murphy wants, he should hang his head in shame!

The biggest crowds is Glasgow's with the Billy and the Tim

With sections of their anti-Christs belting out their vile hymns

Oh they'll go to mass on Sundays or march with their Orange Lodge

Then re-enacting an ancient war that all Scotland has to dodge

Before heading home to batter wives or argue with their son

I've been there in the bad old days and drink only fuels this "family fun"!

Yes they can drink at rugby grounds but their mindset's not the same

That's a million miles away and they go to *watch* a game

Murphy's a teetotaller so why lift this ban on drink?

Is it a decoy or to appease his friends, who find it hard to think?

So while we fight for justice, Murphy takes his rightful place

And confirms what we already know, the man's a waste of space!

Is drinking really their priority, have they nothing else to say?

Labour don't need alcohol to put themselves in disarray.

BBC Question Time.

The Jewels of their empire gathered in disgrace

And rounded on the incomer and got right in her face

The BBC's own Question Time, is a sight you have to see

Especially when the incomer, is head of The SNP.

It was the Heseltine half hour who fought the nuclear cause

A man who needs shaking up with a good kick in the baws

But the nameless Lib Dem reprobate, one I forgot was there

Just seemed to answer nothing and didn't seem to care.

Step forward Duncan Bannatyne, the one from Dragon's Den

Mystified with answers, again, again, again!

And the leader of the liars, who tried to put her down

Just aped her saintly commandant, Miliband the clown

But in all of this, one stood out, with all her answers clear

Our First Minister of Scotland, whom we hold very dear.

She answered with consummate ease and with her usual grace

Though the audience with their chafing words cut through every phase

Undeterred she carried on in her own inimitable way

Concise and clear in everything, she kept the wolves at bay

But common sense is lost on those who cannot understand

Who would rather nuclear missiles were transferred to their land

Who'd want to war with Russia and who'd rob this country's poor

Just to have nuclear weapons, we could never use, outside their very door.

The FM won over adversaries at the UCL this week

Now sixty per cent of English votes don't think her policies so weak

And though most attitudes are changing, the brainwashed still deny

But they just live within their bubble and won't accept they live a lie.

A Typical Scottish Tory Conference.

At The Scottish Tory Conference, there were lines of empty seats

It seems their shepherd's lost some sheep or they're sick of empty bleats

Why do they hire halls for this, is this all for pretend?

For the amount of folk who stay awake, they could use a single end!

They said: He's a cause to condemn and a demon to deplore

And I'm sure the one they refer to, is hurting to the core

Good old Alex Salmond, even though he's now stepped down,

It seems the ghouls of Westminster don't want his ghost around

He's the biggest threat, yet has no seat, but still they're terrified

Of a man whose words were scorned but have since been verified.

They know he's confrontational but know that he's the best

A man of substance and furthermore, they know he will not rest

For he speaks against corruption and wants justice everywhere,

Something, to them, so alien but to him it's right and fair.

One good thing they gave us, was a contract to the Clyde

Eight hundred million smackeroos t to keep 600 folk employed

It may seem a lot of money but it's just our whisky's tax

The amount they steal from Scots each year, and that my friends, a fact.

This British Inquisition is far worse than that of Spain's

No-one now's put to the sword but the poor still die in pain.

Their crimes are not being anti-Christ, they die for just being ill

But suicide is forced on them, this corporate hand of power kills.

The threat of under achieving, means sanctions must be dealt

And the poor are those who suffer as they tweak their money belt.

Tighter yet they draw that string like the noose around a neck

'Til the sinews and the fibres stretch and leave another family wrecked.

The Iceberg.

They leaned upon your counter, one crutch, one missing leg

But you saw only paperwork and watched them as they begged

That human touch we all possess has been traded for results

That ability's been dispossessed, replaced with forms that insult.

Forget hospital appointments, discard that doctor's line

And the operation you're recovering from, tells them you're feeling fine

You're on a drip or comatose but that's also deemed a crime

As those who sanction, eye a clock, that says you weren't here on time.

If communication's paramount, why can't these departments talk

They're all owned by the people, us, yet their doors are shut and locked

They won't speak to one another, saying budgets won't allow

They're understaffed and underpaid yet no sweat shows on their brow.

It's the system that breaks us all, their hands forced in this regime

They've families to feed as well and know these punishments are extreme

But the power that's bestowed on them makes a mockery of control

The real culprit's Ian Duncan Smith, who has no heart or soul.

They listen to excuses but those words they cannot hear

Their clock was ticking loudly, that's the justice we all fear

Their pens were running out of ink through the sanctions they imposed

Three months without a payment – then foodbanks are proposed!

Yes there are those who abuse it, plundering our wealth

Who fake every known illness to prolong their faked ill-health

Who'll take every penny granted with limp and idle hands

They're just as bad as the powers that be, the ones who're in command.

But this is just a pittance compared to the fraud we know goes on

And in the scheme of all things fraudulent, the small fry are but pawns

But two wrongs never made a right, it's the system that has failed

Those who're scratching out a life are being sanctioned, being jailed.

When they mention HSBC's flaws, I look at this iceberg's base

And see corruption everywhere in this regime's golden face

They feed us lies then lie again until most believe it true

Until all accept that lies are lies, they'll do what they always do

The Call of Youth.

You've to work for thirty hours but remember, there's no pay

And for ten more you can look for jobs, do this and have no say

That's our government just telling them, they've no place in this state

And that's just the way they want it, to rule us and dictate.

Placement work, zero contract hours, or like this, working for free

It's slavery in every sense and if they looked up they would see.

They know just what they're doing and say this country must be saved

But that one thinks he's Caesar and his citizens are slaves.

They've overspent, borrowed too much and it's all going as they planned

Austerity's big bucks for them and for the richest in the land,

They've got Iceland down as terrorists because their bankers are in jail

But they're now thriving as a country – we're the ones who've failed.

It's time this self-styled government tore up their self-styled rules

And gave our youth a decent start as soon as they left school

But no, they give them community work with all their hopes destroyed

Doing mundane jobs that should be made full-time to reduce the unemployed

These workers would then pay taxes with the rest to save or spend

And that spend bolsters employment meaning their benefits would end

So with fewer benefits to pay out and our taxes soaring high

And with all these people working, why not give it a try?

But that would smite their greedy fingers in that ever growing pie

There's no cash for them if things go right, that's why they need the poor

And yet detest them as they don't fit in their delusions of grandeur

But the world is growing wise to them as they poison weaker minds

And if protesters stand outside your "house", you just pull down the blinds

Ignorance is bliss to them and apathy's their dream

That absence of emotion which they take to the extreme

They just sit back and tweak their figures then pretend all's great and good

While some poor bastards lying dead, he'd no money to buy food!

Rifkind and Straw.

Farewell Jack and Malcolm, you signed your own death warrants

You helped yourself, just once too much, with crimes we thought abhorrent

You found your own wee banking scam in your land of make believe

 Where all your wishes turned to gold but most of it was thieved!

You exacted total disregard and showed us your true contempt

And proved to us that money talks and that no-one is exempt

You instigated every move with judgements all your own

And now you can contemplate a life of political disown.

But your peers will rally round you like those jolly schoolboys do

You'll get your handsome pay-off with a peerage lined up too

And many more of your misgivings will just be swept aside

For those secret pacts with "funny 'shakes" killed your sense of pride.

You really do not get it, you're caught red-handed and then fuss

We are YOUR supposed lords and masters, YOU answer to US

Politicians are elected by the constituents of a ward

You are paid by them, you're not self employed, I hope I've struck a chord!

One fights his corner then walks out but this blue boy's much maligned

Whilst over in the red corner: He thought! And then resigned!

These naked civil servants, were caught with their pants down

Two caught but they're all at it, and us, we're just the clowns!

An MP can't live on 60 grand, well get another job

You're obviously a high maintenance or else you're just a snob

But last year Straw earned a fortune, half a million if I'm right

And I just hope he paid his tax on this or he's definitely in the shite!

They, of course, had to face the media, like two ageing detainees:

"It's none of your business" Rifkind says, his last words as an MP!

Access for cash – ain't that cute – it's like some dodgy high street shop

But the next shop they'll be visiting, is one that's run by cops!

Just Another Patsy.

Scots voted for a Union and to share the wealth and debt

But the rise of Scottish Nationalists, pose a real and mortal threat;

Is it the death of this democracy or is their grip on it being neutered?

The Times Staff are sadly ill-advised and in need of being tutored!

They dig into the feeblest minds and cultivate the dormant fear

The fear of which has yet to come, the fear they draw so near

They're just another government puppet, trying to help them in their poll

They're just another Patsy and only doing as they're told!

They throw aside the transient waste and lock into futile minds

Expelling all their moral codes, those are memories left behind

They gorge upon a weakness with a strength they know defeats

And sell you their strength of character; deceit is your receipt.

It's the fear of real reporting that's the threat they fear the most

But don't read between the myths they write and reveal the moral cost

They beg, stay in the Union yet immediately condemn

Then by showing their true colours, they're defining us and them.

These rags pit nation against nation, they divide and separate

Much more than YES votes ever could, it's them who write of hate

They won't stand against a government but they'll cover up their lies

And compelled, the feeble minded, will hear their plaintive cries.

The Rise and Rise.

Goods are flying off the shelf, people flock to every store

It's like Christmas on Black Friday with queues right out the door

The staff are all run ragged, there are no zero contracts here

Everyone sweats blood and tears and each one's a volunteer.

Shuffling in and shuffling out, they carry off their goods

And staff will ask no questions in case they're misunderstood

But today when shops are closing down and companies go bust

This is our fastest growing chain and one that should disgust.

Locals signed to local stores, brought on by reforms

No silver ever crosses palms it's all legally done by forms

And though hearts are sometimes heavy, there are smiles all around

You know the shops I'm talking of they're there in every town

Where every creed and every race, every gender, every age

Flock down to their local branch, some embarrassed, some enraged

But a million people last year walked through a hundred doors

You'd think that would be enough but we're crying out for more

And though it breaks their hearts to serve you, it's not them you need to thank

Our governments are responsible, these stores are called Foodbanks.

This coalition's killing us and the poorest need our help

And the greedy who control us, need a right good skelp

These bastards, who're our servants, stick two fingers in the air

Get in there, get it up you, do we look as though we care

We're minted, you're the paupers, deal with it you mugs

You think us little Uni boys but we're the UK's ruling thugs

We're the mask of death a-haunting, the grim reapers in your dreams

We're the central banking system so conform to our regime!

Scrambled.

His eggs are wrapped in Union Jacks and shipped from Harrods, London Town

His "soldiers", to attention stand, 'til he wears his royal crown

Then his solid silver spoon comes down and smashes up the shell

As his scrambled head starts spinning round, locating lost brain cells!

These soldiers are his sustenance and prepare him for his speech

But his audience have "soldiers' brains", out of touch and out of reach

They're either soft and mushy or burnt to cinders like his toast

But they're topped with lashings of his love then served up by the host!

He'll be heading back to Westminster soon, if he can win his seat

But after all the lies he's told, that'll be some bloody feat

If he does, he'll live in Dover House, though he'd rather be in Bute

But it doesn't matter where he lives, he'll bring it into disrepute!

The Devil tells a lie or two and will even buy your soul

And I'm sure the Devil's got a job for him if he's thrown on the dole

He's used to trading places and Old Nick knows his own

But the Murphy man still gives a smile, from his southern Glasgow throne.

He says: These Nationalists are doing me in, they know my every scam

Then laugh when I get angry and watch me throw toys out my pram

They think I'm just an eejit because I don't have a degree

And know I studied for nine years and got my tuition free!

They know who and what I voted for and when I decided to abstain

And that bloody referendum showed, in how many beds I'd lain

Let's face it, I've no future here, it just wasn't meant to be

And if the finger points, with any blame, I'll just say it wisnae me!

YOU Are The Power.

Have we to live our lives in shelter and be a political recluse

We might as well be dead right now with our necks inside a noose

They're all the same, it'll never change, another famous quote

But you, you hold the power, that power's in your vote.

But fear and apathy's so strong, you're afraid to change your ways

Yet you know you're sick to death of things and they're getting worse each day

Things are changing rapidly, look at Scotland, what she's done

You may not like what you see but the people there have won

They've changed the way the people think and have rallied to a cause

A cause that helps the rUK get rid of unjust laws

Do you really want austerity to knock upon your door?

Do we really need these nuclear subs in American driven wars?

When your sons and daughters leave these shores do you think it's just for sun?

How many times have colleagues said: This country's had it, done!

Then some more people say it's great and with a sigh they reminisce

They remember twenty years ago and the good times that they miss

They were younger, freer, better days without the hassle or the stress

And as you look around this land you love, this government's a mess

They're killing Mother Nature here, they're poisoning our land

The toxins from the friends they've bought are getting out of hand

And we're letting them away with it because we're scared of change

We're the same, the normal ones; it's them who are deranged.

Don't let them stamp all over you; it's time you knew your rights

That power lies within your hands and you don't even have to fight.

Two Houses.

There's at least a thousand faces here turned up for the show

Some of them in fancy dress but ask them why and they won't know!

Most of these will fall asleep, some don't even know their name

Welcome, Ladies and Gentlemen, to Westminster's Halls of Shame.

One House has come to vote upon some self-interesting Bill

And the other House will push it through with hands already in the till

Hear, Hear! Ayes and Noes! It's a menagerie, a zoo

And we're relying on these mercenaries to fight for me and you!

Up and down like dancing clowns, the Party leaders set the pace

And the benches hit orgasmic heights with every change of place

It's the politicians battleground, an orgy at its best

While next door in The House of Lords, they're sleeping two abreast!

Back in where the action is, someone's being abused

And the angry sheets of paper fly in the face of the accused

They don't spit blood or clench their fists, their anger is hot air

Any normal guy would say Fuck Off but in here you cannot swear.

They call a truce, it's time for lunch so hand in hand they march

They hit the bar, free of course, those shouting tongues are parched

Then they're back again, at each others' throats, with behaviour so absurd

With all the constant heckling, they can't hear a bloody word!

Order! Order! Comes a shout, from some guy in a big chair

His sarcasm reminds me of some old Music Hall Compere

Clowns to the left of him, jokers to the right

And this guy stuck in the middle is controlling the fights!

If he's the ref who keeps the peace then who makes up the rules?

It's just a public picnic for prim and proper British fools

They abuse the law, abuse our trust, abuse all yet cannot lie

But they can pass a law determining that the most vulnerable may die!

And Lords and Ladies of this land say there's nothing wrong with child rape

The victims should get on with it and get their lives in shape!

Say those in furs with ermine stoles, they're like a cartoon cavalcade

The world is waking up to you, you and your masquerade!

Pure Panic!

This near apocalyptic statement bears down with much belief

That these state backed editorials are intent in spreading grief

Pitting neighbour against neighbour in the most dramatic style

These bigots are responsible for the racist factions in these isles.

Devised and scripted by a state whose hatred must not be diffused

And hope their anti-Scottish followers will detonate their fuse

Their numbing words reveal the truth and show disgusting thoughts

Their love-bombing's all but disappeared; we're now "Incestuous Scots"!

This is one weird cartoon strip, devoid of humour, stripped of wit

In fact, its content's so offensive, they deserve an issued writ!

Oh! How the mighty Guardian's failed, just another fallen rag

Once deemed the prince of papers, their reporters now are gagged

They're too busy licking arses of those protecting paedophiles

But this one just won't go away, they're panicking now in style.

And yet another piece of gutter press to drown Scotland in their flood

"If Scotland rules England, I can foresee the Thames foaming with much blood"

English Members of Parliament in Westminster, total eighty four per cent

And to say that Scots will rule UK, well, that's just a non event!

Yes, they'll fight their case for Scotland for that's who they represent

It's a mindset not an accent without this scandalous content.

They're all in a panic and have informed their press

To sort out these bastards who all voted Yes

They're fucking us up and we haven't much time

Jail them as terrorists or for treacherous crimes

Call that Mark Zuckerberg and let him take a good look

And ban all active Yessers on his precious Facebook

Call out the army and make them secure guards

Surely throwing some Jocks off can't be that bloody hard

And don't let them use nicknames that link them to their land

In fact, ban the whole lot, they're getting right out of hand!

Principles, morals and their social justice for all

Who do this mob think they are, are they rallying to a call?

Is Wallace re-incarnated, has The Bruce come again?

Because all I hear is Hielan' talk and it drives me insane

So in this Union of Equals the threats have returned

One man stoked the fire and his fingers were burned

All jobs in the North will be moved to the South

So it's not just his fingers, we've burnt his sweet mouth

And his allies are with him, they're still there from last year

The same ones who passed, that Bill so austere

But it's down to the people, it's the public who choose

But it seems that corruption means the UK will lose!

Oor Alex.

Alex Salmond, hero, star, is now showing at Leicester Square

And requested by none other than our current Premier!

He sees Miliband from laughing eyes in the top pocket of his suit

And he's aping just what Labour are, a shower of raw recruits!

Did they not realise that bed hopping would add to their despair

But what was Cameron thinking, this confirms Scotland cares

What an advert for the Nationalists at being promoted worldwide

But that effervescent question is: What are they trying to hide?

If he's ridiculing the SNP then I'm afraid it's just backfired

It shows that both are running scared and that was all the Nats desired!

As darkness falls, Oor Alex shines and lights up London's sky

What do Londoners, tourists think, do they just laugh as they pass by?

Are they depriving us of policies as they launch their personal attacks

Or have the policies all dried up with lies and they're papering their cracks

Oor Alex may not get an Oscar for this rudimentary role

But nor will Labour's thespians who are heading for the dole.

He's not even our First Minister, The Man stepped down last year

But it's testament to who and what he is, he's the one they all still fear!

The Tin Hat Brigade.

Some would call them Stalinists, Nationalists or Nats

And the wee lassie that's leading them is wearing her tin hat

Some say she is a Nazi but her name's not Eva Braun

She's the Queen of Caledonia, leading Scotland's bright new dawn.

David "Diddy" Cameron, they're now baying for your blood

And a million angry women want to gie your heid a scud

They don't wear these tin helmets to make themselves look good

They're for hitting guys who have no brains, whose heads are made of wood

It's more than a tin hat you'll need on the day they count the vote

You'll be dreading every word you said when you made that fatal quote

You'll be on your arse and on the dole and, believe me, that's no myth

Cos the bastard who'll make your life Hell will be Iain Duncan Smith

He'll be after you for everything; he'll get right inside your head

He'll be there first thing in the morning and at night when you're in bed

But you've already slept together when you Reds turned to Blue

Karma's such a lovely thing and I'm glad it's come to you.

Whose Weapons for War?

In Iraq a British plane's shot down on its way to arm Islamic State

Weapons made in USA and Israel, this aircraft's only freight

Signed and dated weaponry on the way to kill our men

But will they deny the weapons were on board and send them out again?

We ask for common decency so the starving her can live

Is that too much to ask for because it's not too much to give

But you'd rather deal in arms and watch your wallets swell

But so long as you are happy, the poor can go to Hell.

You block their bare necessities and sanction all the rest

Then shoot them, when they're down and out, and revel in your zest

Don't ever say: "You know what it's like"! You just can't appreciate

What these people feel for you and it's a feeling more than HATE.

You cream the sanctions, cook the books while starvation rules this land

But you know exactly what you do, it's all been schemed and planned

Who's going to fire your nuclear bombs? We'll never see that day

But if we do, they'll be of no use, because we'll all be blown away!

You've cut the armed forces but nuclear warheads will increase

There's no-one to fight your futile wars which you hope will never cease

No naval boats patrol our coast whilst underfunding our frontline

But if corruption keeps your wallets full, then everything else will be just fine!

March of The Puppets.

We get flags fae The Barras for a pound, sometimes less

An' though we can write anything, our favourite word is YES

But if we do they're banned from everywhere even halls throughout oor land

Cos it's a sign of Independence and gets right up their anal gland.

They see it as a sign of treachery but wi' the polis on their side

They can huckle you "for nothing" and throw you straight inside

What is it wi' this country, ane they tell us that they love

They put their hands around you but wear cast iron gloves!

Will you stop slagging off my country, that one you loved last year,

The one above the border, the one the natives hold so dear?

Oor men have puppets in their pockets an' oor wummin wear tin hats

But Pinocchio and his wooden tops don't go in for cheery chats

They're more into dishonesty and involved in major crimes

But if we wave our flags again, it's us who'll be daein' time

We cannae even fly the flag in oor gerdin on a pole

Cos we'll all be jailed, get sacked at work then be thrown on the dole

Or some countryman will burn it but they'll get away Scot Free

And I only hope it changes when Scotland votes for SNP.

That wee lassie wearing yon tin hat, the gallus ane in charge

Her that likes that River City thing, I hope she gies it large

She can wipe out a' they puppets wi' ane lashing o' her tongue

And she can tell they bloody bankers, they'll be getting nae mair bungs

But the men will feel half naked when their puppets have to go

Tae feel the wrath of Westminster when the SNP's on the show.

The Machine.

Our bones are weak, we cannot walk as we learn again to crawl

Our shoulders droop, our saddened eyes, look down to tears that fall,

Our minds and brains are so confused, the tongue it cannot speak

And the smell of toxic waste and gas in the air around us reeks.

The hearts and souls no longer live as they did not so long ago

The heart is beating softer now and it hasn't long to go

Our arteries and veins are blocked, our blood is now congealed

The ears can't hear, the eyes don't see, the lips of truth are sealed.

The machine has taken root in us, we're the assets and their prey

They used, abused and vilified, the people of their day

Then wandered through the people's gold and plotted all their plans

'Til nothing here was left to sell, in this, the people's land.

They ravaged all we had to sell to enhance their pot of gold

Are they the party of the people? It was the people who were sold

But did you sell yourself to them and buy up all their lies

You knew the lies they fed you but you closed your ears and eyes.

You financed their corruption, their monopoly of a state

And now complain of nothing as they take away your fate

You fed into that big machine, in the papers, cyberspace

And somewhere in between you lost a mind you once embraced.

Slowly you forgot yourselves as the system claimed that mind

Then lies on lies became the truth, a truth they hoped you'd find

You're now irrelevant but necessary to those who hold the reins

You're a number to them, nothing more, as your number equals gains.

You're controlled but in denial as you play controller's games

And the controllers, who you'll never know, are the fire in the flames

Burning thoughts that start debates, is an old trick, nothing new

They're all geared up and gift wrapped, a package just for you.

They thought me mad, scorned me and then laughed in their delight

They thought my warnings meaningless when I told them of their plight

We've all been led and still are led with thought put in our minds

But to believe the text they put to us, we really must be blind.

With All Debts Repaid.

I gave you my years but you took all those days

And shoved those precious moments right back in my face

I travelled the country, proudly called out your name

I done all I was asked as you played out your game

But it was the partner you slept with that sickened us all

In the highway of life there are rough roads ahead

And your reliance on apathy, feathered your bed,

We're a country betrayed but it's you who will fall.

You will not die but you are wasting away

And be certain your actions will all be repaid

But I was only a pawn in the game that you played

And Labour, you were, the mistake that I made.

Pools o' Panicked Sweat.

Scots hae fought and Scots hae died

Wi' Borders friends stood side by side

But we hae pasts that ithers hide

Nae North an' South divide.

Can ye feel the rush, the surge, the power

Can ye feel this time, this time is ours

Stand up for a' and dinnae cower

Fae East tae West an' mair.

Dae ye feel the blood rush through yer veins

Did ye feel the hurt an' feel its pain

Take pride in ye for Scotland's gain

Then tell me wha ye are!

Born free an' free we'll stay

Wi' riches mair than some will say

Tell London's hoose we're on oor way

An' no' just ane or two!

The Lords o' power, have us, aye spurned

Yet know not now, which way they'll turn

But turn they have, wi' guilt adjourned

They're at each other's throats!

The empty thrones on stage are set

Ringed wi' pools o' panicked sweat

Aye! But they've seen nothing yet

The man is on his way!

The man whom they have a' chastised

Are incognito, in disguise

That glint's nae longer in their eyes

He's warmin' up his seat!

Spirit!

Oh! The eighteenth of September, that was such a hopeful day

But it was a day when devastation struck and took our hearts away

We were broken but not beaten as tears fell from swollen eyes

But if there's one thing we learned that day, is that the spirit never dies.

Thousands went to Glasgow and proudly stood in Freedom Square

Till the Unionists came marching in and soiled our Scottish air

Attacking locals, tourists, kicking anyone they found

Then they picked on teenage sisters but these brave girls stood their ground.

The loyal police stood watching and showed the world how they had failed

Before marching these young ladies off and slinging them in the jail

But the girls' spirits never weakened and a country they inspired

Rekindling dampened hopes and dreams, our hearts were set on fire.

Carpe Diem, translated, means roughly, Seize The Day

And that's just what we intend do on the Seventh Day in May

Look out traitors of Scotland, "true" Scots who told Scots lies

For the date that I've just mentioned, is the day of your demise.

We hear and see you begging as you blame the SNP

But you're the ones who're begging us, grovelling on your knees

The Scottish people listened to their party of the past

 You've lied to us, we've had enough, this time you've lied your last!

We're steamrolling our country, the same country you betrayed

But we're playing by our rules this time and not the game you played

Your coffin's lying waiting and just needs that one last and final nail

Then the Scotland Branch can raise their sign, "Scots HQ For Sale".

Pat Plunkett.

She's our modern Scottish icon dressed in tartan head to toe

Revered by everyone she's met and loved by all who know

This Yesser of the first degree, even Alex Salmond stands in awe

Of the lady, I proudly call my friend, wee Pat our Indy maw!

She's tenacity, integrity with a verve that won't be shunned

Aye! She may be Scotland's daughter but she speaks for Scotland's sons

She's a Saltire for her Scottish heart; tartan blood runs through her veins

She'll fight for what she thinks is right and her spirit never wanes.

Here's to you our tartan lady, Seventy years under your belt

You've an aptitude for life itself and you're one who won't "Get Telt"

So God help the man or woman who puts this icon down

The wrath of Scotland's watching you and protecting Oor Pat's crown.

Here's tae friends, auld and new and those who can't be here

I raise my glass and make a toast, to Pat, Hope over Fear;

Pat Plunkett, happy birthday, you're a Scottish work of art

Enjoy my Scottish icon, the Queen of Scottish Hearts.

Faulty Towers.

A response so tart in tangled tongue

Like a lawyer's speech with breathless lung

She stammers with her garbled words

Inducing claims that she's absurd.

Consider power, consider minds

Her courtiers wait her direct lines

The empty echoes wait her start

As the etched betrayal pounds her heart.

Like a virgin child she naively stares

At pews so full and busy chairs

The words won't come and knows not why

She wants to curl up and die

But it's not the first, won't be the last

For Kez The Dug is unsurpassed

The glaikit look, the awkward stance

The mouth agog she missed her chance

The eyes have gone the look is blank

But it's not just her we have to thank

There's Jim the gaffer and his gaffes

The one who always makes us laugh

He'll blame the Scots for labour's death

And will until his dying breath

But Labour's death is down to them

They lied to us and were condemned!

Yoo Hoo, I'm Here!

His infamy spans our great divide

They say he'll rob The Thames to pay The Clyde

"Bogle, fiend", I hear them cry

"A Brownie" quipped one passer by!

He's nae man, he's but a moose

Naw! He's the Wallace or The Bruce

Aye! He's the ane they call the Boss

Look! He cerries that St Andrews cross

But I've heard stories, heard some tales

Of how we tried and how we failed

And why The Lord has shared his wrath

Whene'er he shouts Alba gu Brath!

How thousands flock tae hear his speech

And every ear his voice will reach

He's like a Caesar, Emperor, King

They chant his name and start tae sing

Aboot some candle in Iona

Naw! Haud oan there, it's Caledonia

Dae ye think he'll like, well, whit he sees

He wis the Head o' that SMT

Ah heard he wis a monster, a giant, evil man

Who batters guys wi' golf clubs or anythin' tae hand

Ye see he's the ane they tried to wreck

He's the ane they ca' wee Eck!

So Happy Together.

Come join our jovial choir, they say, but don't dare to sing along

Sit down there and listen, we write and sing the bloody song!

This my brothers and sisters is the Loving Family we keep

Well, Wakey! Wakey! Westminster! We're awake and will not sleep.

We've felt The Black Heart of Westminster and listened to your shit

Scotland's re-engaged themselves and you don't like it one little bit

Because what you say we will have and what we actually get

Are memories of false promises which Scots cannot forget.

The Gold, The Banks, The Pensions but most of all the lies

How once you said that Scotland is, your Northern Paradise,

These people are just parasites, pirates sent by Royal Command

Well they make a royal living from their wee Northern Britain's land.

But I'm amazed this little country, is one you hold so dear

Cos it's certainly not the people or politicians we have here

You're all too quick to ridicule every Scottish thing you hear

But it's jealousy you're envious, it's a mentality of fear!

It's a demon that attacks success for you're afraid of what you'll lose

But is this not the democratic way with the people's right to choose?

Your Chancellor, even recently, looked completely out his head

But as he sat in The House of Commons, around him, Britain bled.

While he thought of Blondes and Brunettes with Charlie on the side

He almost doubled up our debts and took all of Britain for a ride

We have Foodbanks now in village halls, that is a disgrace

But Georgie boy ignores it all and powders up his face.

Do you really think he's competent because he's related to the Queen

As you are yourself young Dave, that is nothing but obscene

You've failed here as a premier despite these figures that you quote

For they're all concocted, malleable sums, and you won't get Scotland's vote.

Secret meetings, secret deals, secret rooms by invitation only

The "Vowist" has come back home but home can be so lonely

An honest man can hold his head up high down any street

But this man is a liar and feart of anyone he'll meet.

On the other hand, why do you fear, the one we call "The Man"

Does Mr SNP himself have the power to upset your plan?

We know he's for Independence and Westminster has a fight

But his heart is for the common man and he'll fight for all your rights.

The Rise of The SNP.

Unlike any other in Britain, this was a meeting so vast

That gave hope to its speakers as their public amassed

They wore yellow lanyards and the letters spelt change

For a political meeting which some might find quite strange

But this wasn't some school room but Scotland's grand hall

And when their leader asked for support, they answered her call

Thousands on thousands, now so astute and aware

So proud to be there, this is a country that cares

Every creed, every colour, every sect, every caste

They moulded this Scotland, the final die is now cast.

As each candidate spoke the applause echoed round

As their leader looked on, feet firmly on the ground

They patiently waited for the one they all dread

And then she walked onto the stage, our Lady in Red.

She delivered a speech which was unlike any before

Pundits and plaudits witnessed drowned in the roars

She delivered the words that not only merit this Nation

But all the UK should give this speech a standing ovation

For she spoke not just for Scotland but all the UK

And the crowd let her know in their own special way

Roar after roar, thousands got to their feet

For they too had witnessed an extraordinary feat

They were buzzing, electric, ecstatic, revived

And know from now on the Party will thrive

This crowd listened, dissected and examined words said

As she tore limb from limb the old Party brigade

Now the people have chosen through their cause and concern

Though it seems "the main" politicians are still unwilling to learn

You see, Scottish people remember what most voters forgot

And this change they believe in was hard won by all Scots

Labour's thrown its hand because they know they're despised

By Keir Hardie's country for their treacherous lies

Scots don't forget when those loyal ties are severed

But when it's your own who promise and fail to deliver

It's betrayal at best and it tears your insides apart

But it gave rise to the Party that has Scotland at heart

One that cares about people, especially its own

And the powers at present they want to disown

It's no secret their aim is to set Scotland free

The Nation has spoken, they are now SNP.

Paradise Psalm.

Hush! My friends, go slowly all

And let my words this country sprawl

Tread softly each and every man

And let peasant's ears and foes be banned.

Be wary friends and hide thy face

For if seen, we all, shall fall from grace

God has called for me to preach

And I will give mid-winter's speech

But I'll have no questions, none at all

Discord must leave God's earthly hall

My words will rage but blest are thee

And I will set my people free

With lands so rich, you all will share

In rich employ and sumptuous fayre

With a power held in wealth of dreams

Where emeralds flow in golden streams

Palatial beds will be your berth

Your Heaven can be here on earth

Blaspheme you not, I lay my claim

I stand before you in God's name

And in His house I hereby vow

The time is here, that time is now

Let each man prosper in his town

Or curse the name of Gordon Brown.

Take a Walk.

Come walk with me for just a day and breathe the air I breathe

Walk the streets where I grew up before I chose to leave

Time's moved on but nothing's changed and in cases may be worse

A land so rich was robbed by you, you left Westminster's curse.

Houses, homes are cold and damp which the owners cannot heat

The cupboards have no food in them, they can't afford to eat

To eat or heat's their crisis and one they face each day

And while you say we're better off, the poor just waste away.

The rise of Foodbanks is criminal with some no food to give

Then jail those who "steal" their food from skips just so that they can live!

We keep these people fed and clothed with the little we can spare

We do this because our governments have shown us they don't care.

You want to end austerity but you administer even more

By cutting Welfare payments aimed at crippling the poor

And sanctioning, illegally, those who need the money most

And when you forced staff to stop their cheques, you raised a bloody toast!

Left to fend for months on end, some taking their own lives

Yes with so many headlines hidden the public were deprived

Of your prejudice against the poor and where you get your wealth

Our Health Service is your wealthy mess and you say you care for health!

Degradation, loss of pride they could not carry on

Every night they go to sleep but awake to their same dawn

When will you tax the rich and companies who evade?

The Scottish public see right through you, their poverty's man made.

I will stop zero contracts hours, words from the infamous Tony Blair

He said that twenty years ago to show us how much he cared

Now Miliband is telling us how he'll carry on Blair's fight

By agreeing with more Tory cuts going against the poorest's plight.

You want to end austerity yet Ed Balls wouldn't change a thing

Oh Labour you are useless and brought on this Highland Fling

People here are dancing in every street and every town

For Queen Nicola of Caledonia now wears our Scottish crown.

Hell for Heaven.

Begone thy sleekit silver tongue, you speak as though we're deaf

We list no more to velvet prose where phrases lead to theft

Where humanity is measured by your weight of stolen gold

Where leaders cling together for fear of losing all control

Of what they cherish selfishly or of losses they'll incur

Instead you ridicule at ease with your denigrated slurs

The people whom you say you love, you are abusing your employ

But we hear your careless whispers seeking only to destroy

Our knowledge is all growing and silenced cannot be

This indignant sufferance cannot be endured but no more you'll hear our plea

Does your god protect the saintly knights and cast aside their slaves

Self proclaimed dictators whose directives end with graves

These Incumbents seek ascendancy to their god that lives in Hell

But when their Armageddon comes, it's there that they shall dwell.

Allegiances to olden ways to bloody kingdoms won and lost

Have brought their own destruction and still we bear the cost

Only then will true justice rule, only then will we be free

For if Labour was my conscience past, let it now be SNP.

What's A Bomb Between Friends?

If you don't agree with illegal wars, or renewing nuclear bombs

Or razing countries to the ground whilst people sing their psalms

Or whilst bombs replace our cash for health as our children go without

The mercenaries are those in charge, of that I have no doubt.

But they won't fight, they send the fools, send in the bloody clowns

The only ones who're brave enough to turn their fortunes round.

They manipulate your very mind in their game, called conquer and divide

They bear the cost, you're profit, 'til you've killed and then you've died.

Their re-commissioned bombs on trucks surge through Scotland's streets

And disregard all weather warnings from the MOD's elite

They're all in it together, right up to their filthy little necks

But the web they weave is broken, but, is still virile and complex

First we break illegal wars and fabricated foes we always fight

Then we claim our sovereignty and retrieve all our legal rights

And lastly Independence which was taken from our hands

Hands tied by these profiteers who still profit from this land.

Wresting Chains.

Come feel the power held inside,

Come feel it deep within

We're harnessing oor future here

Let that future now begin.

Feel the pride aboon us a'

That rallies 'roon this nation

This time we'll rise an' no' fa' doon

An' be oor ain salvation.

We hae lain far too long

An' hidden fae oorsels

But we hae seen the power here

Tae break Westminster's spells.

Fae Cambuslang tae Tomintoul

There's treason and divide

But there's a light in a' o' us

That keeps our spirits blithe.

Take yer stand an' be the man

And use your sovereign power

Be that man ye want tae be

An' take back what is ours.

Hear the silence fae the land

The land that's taken fae us

There's such a hush but wait for it

That voice is rising up fae a' us.

Rise an' rise Scots ane an' a'

Rise to Freedom's call

And when we wrest the chains fae hearts

Then Freedom comes tae a'.

Blood and Ink.

Craft me not a blade of steel

But furnish me a quill

And I'll cast out ten thousand men

Yet not one shall I kill

The butcher's mind is blocked of sense

Death is all he sees

But I will dip my quill in ink

And sign for victory.

No thundering forth horse-laden knights

Will gallop through my head

No, I will take my lively queen

To comfort me in bed

My sweat will not be that of fear

Intent on deathly fight

No, I will break my fast by dawn

Then sign with all my might.

The Man From Newhouse.

Though his house and hamlet may be gone

His name and fame the world has spawned

Yet his "birthplace" sign hangs wrongly on

The house he never knew.

In a tenement the great man lived

And to this world his all he'd give

But you! He never could forgive

You turned your back on him.

To his beliefs you would not adhere

To the faith the great man held so dear

His hopes you traded with your fear

You took the selfish path.

He attended night school aged just ten

Where he traded shovel for the pen

But by day he mined the pits like men

A boy beyond his years.

He sought justice for the common man

And not just those who mined the land

This rebel fought those in command

He would not play their game.

He arranged strikes 'til he got his way

The men o' muck got better pay

The Agitator had won the day

His next stop was Parliament.

In Westminster he wore his tweeds

To wear the black suits they'd decreed

But our non-conformist disagreed

And wore a deerstalker to boot!

His policies have stood the test of time

And witnessed socialism's climb

But this Labour favours all war crimes

He was a pacifist.

Cumnock town hold his remains

But in his grave he'll feel the pains

Of the movement that's shown him disdain

Keir Hardie: The greatest ever Labour man.

Men Overboard!

When will you stop these tweets of hate

Or jealousy because of one debate

Defeatist measures, lies from truths

Come only from the most uncouth!

They're politicians I hear you say

So they lie! It's always been that way,

It's what they do to get things done

And they all play this game just for fun

So if all their truths are based on lies,

Does the one who lies best take the prize?

But they've forgotten half of what they've told,

Their memories lined with thoughts of gold

And can't find words to please our ears

Are all our Leaders gripped with fear?

Too many lies have caught their tongues

Or too busy thinking of their bungs

From their industrious corporate friends

Who rely on all these stupid trends

That spread around the Twitter posts

Heard and leaked by some French Ghost

These games they play are just for fun

But we're the ones who're being done.

Oh yes! They're scared, they've all to lose

And now it's time for us to choose

Tory, Labour, Ukip, Lib-Dem

It's your choice, pick one of them

Or vote for Plaid Cwmru or Green

Or Nicola's SNP Machine

It's time to smash Westminster's hold

And the sinking ship that's made of gold!

The Apathy of All.

Treat every word conspicuously for they treat yours with contempt

It is they who show the apathy and to do so are content

Labour proved that point with Scots, in fact everywhere they've stood

They make it clear they've understood but clearly have misunderstood

"Make it Clear", a strange old phrase as though they're up to their little tricks

And the ease with which they all agree is enough to make you sick.

Thank god we've "little" parties who have rocked their golden boat

But I'm sure they're not so thankful for "taking" all their votes.

We've French letters made in Scotland and they connive to say it's true

Even though it's been disproved, there's always one who'll misconstrue

Whose reputation takes a daily dive with everything he says

Yes! It's Alistair Carmichael folks, our own Scottish Secretary

And the stupid bias media who hire fools to write their news

Ask questions without thinking then report distorted views

About those nasty CyberNats and how vile they have been

He may be the best at the BBC but James Cook's views are obscene

But let's not stop at Jamesy boy, let's dig out Andrew Neill

The man who rules our airwaves with so much to conceal

The pompous would be politician who's both arrogant and rude

Rips into those just like him and yet at times colludes

And sometimes I can't blame him, I'd lose my bloody head

But they all sit at the same table to share their daily bread!

Then there's Scotland's rise of the SNP is down to Scotland's love of gays

A comment so ridiculous and yet David Torrance looks for praise

It's laughable to say the least and deplorable at best

But at least when Independence comes, we can put them all to rest!

Who's The Threat?

He's nothing to show and nothing to hide

Nothing up top and nothing inside

The brainless one should stop and think

Or is Carmichael's brain the missing link?

He'll languish with the rest of those

And get himself a healthy dose

Of what it's like being on the dole

For trading his immoral soul

To this nation's deeper, darker force

Who deal in all without remorse

These aides reflect their show of fear

But show no guns or bandolier

But stealthily behind a gaze

They play the tune of he who pays

They sit and pry behind a screen

In the comfort they remain unseen

But it's us, our nation, I believe

They contrive to delude, deprive, deceive

But this country should have no regrets

For our wee SNP's their biggest threat!

The Power Lord.

Rebuked and rebuffed then firmly put in his place

By three of his masters with, all four, a disgrace

He'll continue to lie even though he knows he's wrong

And he'll just carry on singing his wee Branch Office song.

He contradicts and contravenes every moral known to man

He has ideals that are all his own in his own idyllic land

I'm convinced he is a lunatic, a rocket who's completely off his head

And he's the reason here in Scotland HIS Labour party's dead.

Every speech he makes backfires but the secretary's undeterred

He won't admit or show it but this man is running scared!

He has power over nothing and definitely no financial clout,

Yet believes he is a power lord and loves to act it out

He shouts for Bonnie Scotland but who's he trying to kid

He is governed by a puppet and does just as he's bid!

Magrit.

Tell me how does it feel to betray all your friends

The salt of the earth here in Glasgow's east end

How could you betray them, it just doesn't make sense

But Magrit, don't worry, you've been well recompensed.

You're only a fool who flaunted your rules

And dined with the best of them dripping in jewels

But as you dined with the lords and the ladies of muck

You forgot all your friends 'til you ran out of luck.

Have you no pity, no guilt or no shame

As you look 'round your table for someone to blame

But it's you Margaret Curran who deserted your friends

You think you're upmarket, you just don't comprehend.

You can better yourself but the good's deep inside

It's put there so you, from yourself, you can't hide

You betrayed that old self for a coin in your purse

You're part of the parcel that bowed to Westminster's curse.

In the tenements darkness there is dampness and cold

Where a single light shines with its softness of gold

But midnight or daylight or dusk through 'til dawn

The name of their "friend" will soon be history, gone.

Then the east end will flourish though it might take some years

But will you still be dining with your like, with your peers

They pay for your luncheons when some of them cannot eat

No wonder you're snubbed as you walk down their street.

They begged you to help them but you chose to deceive

So up stepped another who asked them to believe

You blamed all those rich friends who are living down south

There's less rubbish in landfill than comes out of your mouth.

As the tenements sleep with the poor folk inside

Their purse may be empty but they're bursting with pride

But you, Margaret Curran, you are already dead

And your friends have assured us you've a heart made of lead.

You can rest on your laurels when your final bell tolls

Reminiscing with friends you're still trying to control

Just a lady in waiting with the glory days gone

But with colleagues still conning her façade carries on.

Extinction!

Do the poor here exist for the rich man's command?

We've had a century of this arrogance and still it rules this land

Where the media, through their bias, refuse to criticise

And will they wait upon their funeral when, at last, the party dies.

These coffins lie in wait, laid open, stark and bare

Empty for the moment but their stars will soon be there

As rosettes ruffle in the northern wind, they gather here today

The sombre coats, soaked by rain, they clasp their hands to pray.

And as the hearse moves slowly forward, the silence brings on tears

But a nation celebrated, their hopes had conquered fear,

The massacre was waiting; and the people chose the time

Sweetness would be their revenge, they'd be punished for their crimes

One by one they crumbled and one by one they fell

Yet again they would not listen and confined themselves to Hell

The people are the power and they can give or take away

And damned will be the tyrants who see us as their prey.

Only One Woman!

They seek to amuse us with hatred, I suppose that's what criminals do best

But the most dangerous woman in Britain, has told them to "gie it a rest"

Yet this hatred in Unionist parties shows that at last they are taking some heed

Of a party who speaks for the people and regardless of colour or creed.

She is hated by those in denial, the same "those" who fight for our cause

The same "those" who sanction to kill off the poor and still they hang back for applause.

Repetitive words keep on coming, the tin hat's Britain's great threat

Cos she's stealing their riches to give people life while dragging the poor out of debt

But their democracy's come back to haunt them and right away they're on the back foot

Herr Major, the grey man delivers to our country, his speech with a Nazi salute!

But this innovative woman called "Sturgeon" has turned politics up on its head

And if you think us Nazis, as Unionists do, please look to queen Lizzie instead

Sax-Coburg and Gotha now Windsor, forced into their war change of name

Afraid of the people she reigns over yet it's still Britain's people she blames.

Oor Nicola's brighter than sunlight and shines when she's up on that stage

And when she gives her equality sessions, the Unionists feel only rage

It's Better Together for bankers and crooks, the rest they hoped we'd forget

Like promises, Vows – numbered 1, 2 and 3 but for now it's as good as it gets.

They love the thought of Trident's renewal, but these people have no heart or soul

The idea of extinction appeals to them all but they're too scared to take final control

Bombs, death, destruction and poverty, they want this and says it makes sense

But Oor Nicola's got more in her arsenal and that tin hat's not her only defence

She has power they only can dream of and an army who'll stand for their rights

And if truth is the ultimate weapon then they're in for a helluva fight!

It's not only Scotland who love her, though they don't tell you that on TV

But if Facebook and Twitter are credible sites then the UK would vote SNP!

Outlandish!

They're only there to prime the fuse but this could seal the Union's fate

These patronising sentiments promote their anti-Scottish fuelled hate

Fragile words and testaments incriminate once again

And there is much severe fragility in these words of frightened men.

They rejoice with sighs of great relief but their doubts are always there

Their squirming skin's a slimy mess in a cesspit that's all theirs

But all this sentimental bullshit brings with it the real danger of division

A sentiment that either brings deep despair or ecstatic wild derision!

They paint a Jacobean Scot where kilts and Claymores swish and swirl

Dancing to a highland air where drunkards wheech and birl

And the Haggis, sorry terrorists, roam through Westminster floors

Unlocking with their sgian dubhs what goes on behind closed doors.

These all singing, all dancing troubadours plot in Freedom Square

Reliving referendum days with their Saltires in the air

Rallying for social justice as they voice their need for change

Whilst headless politicians are left baffled and deranged.

In this democratic country that word spells treachery and fear

And the terrorists they say they love, they wish they weren't here

These Fascist scum should just sit down and shut their Nazi mouths

But try telling that to Scotland's people who are rampant north to south.

The Innocents.

Can you still show no compassion for the blood between your fingers

A memory congealed in nails, its putrid smell still lingers

And the hand that killed the baby of some old and ancient mother

Cries yet beside her daughter's tears for an only son and brother;

A pillow's just a comfort in the dark.

You suffocate in shadows as you plant seeds in our midst

That grow into a quest for truth that we know can't exist

For you cover all those flowers so they never see the sunlight

Surrounding us with fantasy like the ladies of the night;

Poison's always present in your life.

You think you walk on water like some emperor once so great

And cast your spell like fishermen in your slavish polit state

But then when you are drowning and the water wraps around you

Do you think your victims worry as they're smiling out of view;

The bullet comes in many shapes and forms.

These children of the sunshine were just playing in their garden

Boys and girls laughing then you stopped it without pardon

These children lie awake at night while mothers cry in bed

A universe of children's tears but the living are the dead;

Rest in peace the angels of the stars.

This world is seeing evil, all brought on by fellow men

As the innocents look down and see it happening again

But the gambler smiling wryly deals himself another hand

As the black ace falls on someone else's land;

Red sands only happens where there's gold.

Skribbles.

(To the genius that is Michael Larkin).

He marches to their tuneful sound

And watches all the folk around

He looks at different clothes they wear

Their banners flying in the air

And thinks, before they disengage,

Last orders, encores, on the stage

So holds his placard up on high

Depicting folks that soon will die,

The art of this young soldier never dies.

He seems footloose and fancy free

And laughs at them through artistry

His colours mixed before they're bought

The paint on palette, brush in pot

His brush strokes, quick, come down upon

A canvas that his hero's on

Sketched in haste with fine detail

Or heroine he cannot fail

A Skribble turned into a masterpiece.

This joker, clown, he's one and all

From club and bar he'd nightly fall

The stranger gets into his mind

You know him but your eyes are blind

Is he the one you used to be

When you were young and all was free

The charmer takes his chance in life

And casts aside the grief, the strife

Then from his mind he paints his tapestry.

From dawn 'til dusk he slaves away

His concentration cannot sway

He's almost spent it's after dark

These charcoal lines have made his mark

But man's best friend is by his side

The board is up, the paint has dried

But Unionists see his work a farce

45% My Arse!

His words speak more than actions ever could.

He dreams in Scottish colours

With his strokes of Independence

A master of his own free will

He sees his work a penance

For the free land that he's seeking

He's the ghost behind salvation

Seldom heard but often seen

He strives to free his nation;

The artist's stroke can paint a thousand words.

To the warmongers and criminals

Who rape the land we love

He's reliant solely on his art

With no help from above

And from a silent era

He holds aloft his plaque

A million words crammed into few

Where a bright line shines from black,

He paints the thoughts that no-one else can see.

A Drink in Freedom Square.

(To all who've been, you'll know these words).

I had a drink, well one or two

Then one or two again

Then had again my one or two

All with my fellow men

We wandered in and wandered out

And watched the banners fly

Then in and out and back again

And met some passers-by.

Hello my friend, my name is Paul,

I've come to Freedom Square

Will you join me in a drink or two

And then go back for mair

Come have a drink with me my friend

The first one it's on me

And raise a glass to good folk here

And end austerity.

So out we went where people sang

And danced and clapped their hands

And the music that they listened to

Was to free their nation's land

They came fae north and east and west

And from the south they came

To play their part in history

And all in Scotland's name.

The highland laddies played a tune

The highland lassies danced

Then an Englishman took to the stage

By Christ he took a chance

But loved he was by one and all

And cheered by every hand

It was Chunky Mark who came tae us

To save his English land.

He said the land he came from

Had ceased to show their care

Well, he should bring them all to Glasgow town

To dance in Freedom Square.

And still they danced and still they sang

And still they clapped their hands

Then all went home and had a drink

Tae their bonnie, bonnie land.

The singers sang, the speakers spoke

And people's views were aired

So if you want a dance or two

Come down to Freedom Square

A voice for Scotland was the cause

Twelve thousand came to hear

But the whole Square just erupted

When he sang Hope Over Fear.

The tears were flowing thick and fast

When the singer sang his song

If you'd no tears, you were not here

Or you did not belong.

So powerful the words he sang

With passion and with flair

He captured all within that song

Today in Freedom Square.

No More.

(Written after Boris Johnson's alleged threat to ban
the bagpipe from the streets of London).

So silent will be London's streets

No more the pipes will play

No more the eerie haunting sound

By night time or by day

No more the jig, the reel, lament,

No more the kilted soldier

No more the Scots will proudly dress

With the pipes slung o'er shoulder.

The skirl that led us into war

You'll hear again no more

But hear you will a'thing else

From any foreign shore

No more will you hear or see

Our pipers play an air

For we are Scots, and proud of that

But you've a racist London Mayor.

A "Black" Day.

Dear Douglas Alexander, I just had to write these lines

I know it's not that easy to pretend that all is fine

But each day I read the papers and know you're under some duress

But I'm so glad Scottish Labour is in such a bloody mess

You see all your Paisley Buddies, have all had enough of you

You didn't heed a word they said or heard their points of view

You pose for Labour photographs with your cardboard cut-out fans

That you've drafted up from England in your mercenary vans

Who you put in bed and breakfast then roam with you for hours

And make them swap their T-shirts to show your party's muscle power

It started last September when you humped your friends in blue

So your lack of seats in Scotland is entirely down to you

You tried your best to bury Scots but forgot we're hardened seeds

And here in Spring we're blooming and we're rooting out the weeds

For all you see is money and into self annihilation

Self harming, self destruction, in some weird political castration

So I do not write to sympathise for the grief you have to bear

Because for sixty years you lied to us, pretending that you care

And I pray to god wee Mhairi Black gets aboard that Euston train

And fight for all her Buddies whom you showed nothing but disdain

She may only be a student and at only twenty years of age

But I hope when she's elected, you'll at last feel Scotland's rage!

Yours Sincerely!

Lord Janner.

He may have dementia but what of his crimes

To the boy who's now a young man

Can he remember, the boy surely does,

Or was it all just part of a plan?

Each day brings a sadness and messes with life

But he really just wants justice done

And as he looks back in years, harbouring fears

His hopes have dwindled to none!

Each day that passes, he hopes and he prays

Those memories will be erased

But the wizard of love, the great god above

Says compassion has seen better days!

In this paedophile Britain, they trawl every floor,

Watching from every closed door

Every nook, every cranny, as you walk to your home

They're hoping today they will score.

They'll never plead guilty and be never accused

Of the young they're deemed to abuse

The judge and the jury, they're one and the same

They confirm he's paid all his dues

It just doesn't make sense, he claimed his expenses

Does his memory work when it suits

He's lined all their pockets and walked off Scot free

Corruption is for the astute!

Red Are Dead!

His contorted face reminds me of a painting by Picasso

And his thoughts are even weirder as he preaches them in Glasgow

Rabbie Burns had Holy Wullie but I'm stuck with Creepy Jim

Who stands on his plastic pulpit belting out his holy hymns.

I hope tae Christ we never get him cloned!

Do not the scriptures tell us that beyond the northern wall

The heathen nations co-exist to bring about our fall

Where painted maidens rally and blaspheme our prophecies

Satanists and anarchists who are politically diseased

That Unicorn's a lot to answer for!

He holds aloft a manuscript from his phantom house of power

The charismatic secretary is near to zero contract hours

He's shaking uncontrollably and trembling like a leaf

But as he's banging nails in coffins he cries out in disbelief

No-one loves a liar anymore!

This dying minstrel quavers as he sings us his swan song

This phoenix who arose to tell Scots just where they all belong

Cast out these heathen nationalists and put them to sword

All this from one Jim Murphy who fucked the nation he adored!

Rest In Peace, your office here is dead.

This Christendom.

Goad him not nor vex him

Nor his appetite whet

For lords of war are in pretence

And covet only debt.

For on your knees he needs you

Mere peasants in his name

He plies his words in deadly game

And jests that he is lame.

He stays abed and flirting wench

Begs him kindly for

A morsel for a mouth or two

Whilst her husband fights his war.

She feeds him well to gain a meal

But knows she is indebted

Now he controls the handsome wench

one, this fox has vetted.

Lay down your body, bare your soul

And let your lord be pleased

And let me spread my princely seed

Whilst you beg on your knees.

Triumphant, he'll be once again

Whoring with his hold

But the taste of fair and handsome flesh

Does not compare to gold.

He took your free and willing love

In agreement with your trade

But remember it was only you

Who chose the bed you made.

These lords they play with time itself

Their evil trade they ply

Their wealth must come before your health

For peasants serve then die.

So simple and beguiled they

That live in deep despair

But the evil lordship welcomes all

Who cometh to his lair.

A mistress for his every need

His bed's their only bet

These witless wonders little know

Their debt's already set.

He solicits only for himself

And politicises crime

But when a serf bows to his lord

Their debt is for all time.

Miliband.

That little sanctimonious pompous prick, Labour's head of staff

Showed disrespect beyond belief which was certainly no gaffe

A premeditated answer told Scots just where he stood

With the arrogance and ignorance he keeps for Holyrood!

He just fucked the Labour movement with one utterance from that mouth

With the most undemocratic answer to appease those in the south

But it was the arrogance and ignorance applied to what he said

This statement for and to the people, who've been loyal, sixty years

A high risk tactic thought out well, that will only end in tears!

Are we the ones they used to love, rebellious kilted upstarts

They've chastised and they've ridiculed every sovereign Scottish heart

He's another who thinks loyalty is come upon each day

So may blackened nights become your days as you die in disarray!

Your monuments will topple and your temples crushed by those

Who, in your democracy, you vehemently oppose

Not just oppose but demonise like a master with a rule

But Ed, WE ARE YOUR MASTERS and not delinquents at your school!

OUR POWER which is held from us, by the squeamish and the weak

But if you ignore the Scottish voice, you will then hear that voice speak

Your sheets of treason are still warm, that bed remains unmade

And it'll take more than a chambermaid to right those wrongs you made!

You slipped in through the back door to avoid your voters from the past

And in the dear green place that's Glasgow, a different vote they'll cast

You see, YOU'RE the reason Scottish Labour's dead and Scotland's voting SNP

And the votes, if some were borrowed, well those, you'll never see!

Hope.

I beg you do not grab my wrists

And bind me with your rope

But let me loose so I am free

To fill your minds with hope

And when the eye has cast its gaze

And taken in the view

Then hope, you'll feel, within your mind

My honest gift to you.

Feel it sweep and cleanse your mind

And lift your harnessed heart

This birthright, which is rightly yours,

Let no man take apart

The chains are only in your mind

Your heart is your command

And listening to the pride that beats

Will conquer their demands.

Let no one infiltrate your mind

Or manipulate your thoughts

Be honest with who you really are

Don't let your dreams be bought

Let the golden sands of time run through

The hope you feel inside

And may your heart forever more

Feel this burning pride.

All these gifts I give to you,

Where your forebears made their name

The richest prize that's known to man

A place that they called "hame"

So now pay homage to that name

And grasp with unfettered hands

For what was theirs is yours this day,

This, the bonniest of lands.

SNP in Westminster.

They may not have the expertise, primed rhetoric or experience

Or accredited with the etiquette of those who fail in their deliverance

But they've an educated rawness, a freshness, and a zest for all that's good

And been guided by our finest right here in Holyrood.

Don't let their lies, injustices, overcome what you think is right

They will cleverly, in polit mind, seek to blight and blind your sight,

Nothing will deter the beast that lives inside that evil, twisted mind

They live by the rules of a time long gone, that persecutes mankind.

They'll bend their own agenda like a lawyer takes his brief

And like whores corrupt your virgin thoughts which beggar their beliefs

They're the ones who pray to gold in all its shapes and forms

And cleanse their guilt, ain't that the truth, by adding more reforms.

They're against their infirm public and blame some motive for the change

Deflecting all inadequacies confirming elitists are deranged

Each one so alien, and untypical of, the ones they represent

But the panic in their squabbling sounds the death toll, they are spent!

They're disabled in their corrupt minds if they accept the status quo

And they struggle with the powered rise from an electorate who know

Respect comes with a hefty tag: The cost of being true!

True to your country, true to yourself and true to me you.

Only then will the people's voice be heard, only then will they respect

A nation they thought silent, ignorant, and chose only to neglect

You failed us all so many times it has led to your Scots'

demise

But there will be a coalition with some form of compromise.

Fundily Mundily.

(A Tribute to Jim Murphy).

A man who lies – or so says Ruth

But in fairness, Jim's lie is the truth

He's just a man who thinks he's right

But we all know he talks utter shite!

Even Bill and Ben have put him down

"Fundily Mundily"? What a clown

He gets muddled up, gets on our tits

And builds houses out of benefits!

That's the social housing side now done

This manifesto game's some fun

Then dances round like some demented twat

With two ladies doing The Alley Cat!

His head's a Magic Roundabout

And he's the star, I have no doubt

And when Zebedee says Boing! Time for bed

Big Fundily Mundily rests his head.

Jim's a dreamer but still a creep

And every dreamer needs his sleep

He'll dream of being our new FM

"FM" Fundily Mundily, what a gem!

The Darkest Side of Jim Murphy.

It left some angry and few in doubt

But now those few must get him out

An orchestrated meet in town

Designed to put the SNP down

He's a Tory in Red Labour's skin

And says he cares for kith and kin

Yet this man stands for all we hate,

He's a quisling sealing Labour's fate.

He's a neo-Tory against free speech and will abolish Human Rights

He's acting out his humane role and only his rights are the rights he fights.

He's a prominent politician and stands elected to a most unethical board

Of The Henry Jackson Society, which the Labour party has deplored

And though the leaders begged him leave, Jim Murphy holds that special place

In a Society formed to rule supreme and for this alone should be disgraced.

His role, advisory councillor, conniving with his Conservative friends

Convinces me, that his loyalty lies, in the controlling power of men.

He's not just here for recompense nor under some strange false pretence

He knows exactly what he does with no scruples, principles or moral sense

His credibility lies in tatters, his political life a total mess

Is his Armageddon calling him, has he robbed us to excess

The Henry Jackson Society, exists, for the elite's supremacy

But this man will just soldier on and dumps on us this legacy.

The Indy Girls.

They've shown us how to play the game

And their name has gained these girls fame

They felt defeat so tell me why they're grinning

They lost the battle not the war

Independence is what they're fighting for

A peaceful war, that they're intent on winning.

The others run without their pride

And always make time on their side

Or so they think, controlling what they're after

But The Indy Girls have a view

They're fighting here for me and you

And in the darkness I can hear their laughter.

Somewhere there's a crowded room

Where friends' words mix with sweet perfume

The gloves are off, the main event is nearing

With the blues detested in this land

And the red pretenders thrown their hand

The yellow corner's the one that they are cheering.

They're sincere, against austerity

Debating with integrity

These ladies love the sacrifice they share

Across their nation Saltires fly

Where dreams are real and hopes are high

True friendship is the only cross they bear.

Will Scotland think of Scotland's past

They know the country's fate rests in their hands

In hopeful eyes a fire burns

They know this nation's always spurned

And at last a voice will be heard from their land.

If you're at a rally they attend

They'll embrace you as a new found friend

Their army just seems to grow and grow

But to get to know how these girls think

You'd better join them for a drink

And if they ask you, you'd better not say No!

The Big Day 7th May 2015!

Their game of chess commenced at dawn

Their battle swords so feebly drawn

But who was king and who was pawn

Oor people showed nae care!

Their hearts were pounding, pumping fast

Wi' sleepless nights but maist the last

But wi' passion, pride, they a' amassed

Tae put their country first!

The atmosphere was tense and fraught

But spirits here were not distraught

A lesson here had tae be taught

And their tutors thronged the streets!

Oor streets may not be paved wi' gold

But we are proud and rightly bold

Yet turn on us and we will scold

Ye'll feel the wrath o' Scots.

This country you said you endeared

Yet behind oor backs you laughed and sneered

Can ye smell the stench of rotting fear?

Saor Alba gu Brath!

We're a nation loyal and devout

But a' yer words sowed seeds o' doubt

And the banners cried Red Tories Out

Farewell, ye had yer chance!

Scotland's daughters and her sons

Saw justice here was rightly done

Yer love and hate was a' undone

They voted wi' their hearts.

SNP and History.

We witnessed every Scottish voice, give out a Lion's roar

And, united, shouted Scotland's voice, austerity no more

Scotland last night made their choice to be almost Westminster free

By rejecting all their promises and by voting SNP.

As the realisation dawned on them, their SNP were gaining seats

Sheer ecstasy brought on floods of tears that flowed through Scotland's streets

Not one or two but fifty six and only three escaped their wrath

Democracy marched out last night and built a bright new yellow path.

This was not an easy task but Scotland done their people proud

The massive scalps that fell today means Scotland's voice is loud

And as the nation's map turned yellow, tears flowed at that as well

They tore apart The Red Tories' grip and sounded their death knell.

This wasn't just a victory but near annihilation

We felt the yellow sgian dhubs cut them from our nation:

Labour; take a good look in your mirror as you stare up at your sky

From the many coffins laid out here when your Scottish comrades died.

Save some words for our leader who's only seven months in the post

Now a world renowned politician and the pride of Scotland's toasts

Intelligent, compassionate but with the fight of any man

And last night proved to her people, she's the one to lead our land.

She's a woman without equal and a manner so pronounced

Her aspirations more than realised, their domination trounced

She led us to a victory with a determination to succeed

And with unprecedented loyalty from those loyal to her creed.

And lastly for our people who showed such courage, fight and grace

They showed elitist governments that their voice is not misplaced

I'm not too sure a lot of them will read these words I write

They're probably curled up in bed after partying through the night.

To each and every one of them, I salute you one and all

You had the guts, the grit, belief and in truth you had the gall

To tell all Scotland's "givens" exactly what you think

And if you haven't had a shwally yet then pour yourselves a drink!

Duracell.

Resignation, resignation, with more and more commiseration

But he who led now wants to lead a party thriving in stagnation

He has no seat, he has no hope and lastly has no shame

He's the charismatic one and I'm sure you know his name.

The man who jogs in Scotland shirts and remonstrates from crates

The man whose tongue must never stop and whose lungs do not deflate

The robotic man, does he need breath, is he battery controlled?

But does it really matter now he's just another doled!

One Big Bumpy Ride.

We won't be a silent majority and won't get back in that box

We won't be the quiet sensation and hide under embarrassment's rocks

We love conversation in all that you say, some just love to speak

And you've come at a time, sadly for all, when their voice is nearing its peak

For the bricks in your big house are rotten, crumbling, ready to fall

The political tremors are rumbling with words that speak for us all

Scotland has spoken with passion and will live with all of your fears

For the promises made unto Scotland, mostly fell onto Scottish deaf ears.

We know our rights and you know we are right, believe us, you're in a state

We care with a passion and willing to fight and deny you austerity's fate.

No, we won't lay down like numpties and accept everything you've got to say

There are riots going on across London and no-one is going away

There's unrest in all of our nations and marching against all your cuts

For the slim majority you're governing with has no room for ifs or buts.

The electorate chose you their champion, to represent them, not to dictate

And don't rule as though you're the king of kings in some ancient biblical state

But nor is this the Victorian age where the illiterate poor consent

There's anger marching on your doorstep as protesters show their discontent

You're only three days into office and already tensions fill streets

They witnessed your first five years and won't accept any repeats.

If unity and fairness is what you seek then why conquer and divide?

Us and them! Rich and poor! Ahead lies, one big bumpy ride!

The People's SNP.

Walking tall, I see you are now. Why not take a bow

Home Rule here will soon be coming. Fuck yer fuckin' vow!

Fifty six tae Labour's ane, it wisnae hard to see

Add the Tory and Lib-Dem, that gie's them fuckin' three!

Glesga's people's mair than happy, Labour's oot the door

We're fillin' it wi' yellow suitsand tartan shoes galore!

The poor wee kids will eat at last,this new mob urnae crooks

But you, you bastards, scoffed their lunch, then cooked the fuckin' books!

Tae oor wee gaffer, take a taxi. No thanks; I'll take the bus

Nae limousine for Nicola, she's shown she's ane o' us!

Here's tae a' an' here's tae them,the anes like you and me

Raise yer gless an' make a toast:

Tae the people's SNP!

Expectations.

Are our expectations credible, have we set our sights too high?

Will the rawness of our rookies, be cast out like passers by?

Are they capable of competing? Are they regarded as a force?

Their self belief answered back with the stoutest words; of course!

As they graced the steps of Westminster, in awe but what a sight

The pride that stood for Scotland, there, was one of sheer delight,

And I bet their minds were buzzing with hearts that felt so proud

They'd made it and promised us, Scottish voices would be loud

And our aspirations, whilst realistic dreams, have yet to be achieved

But the expertise of polished minds have Scots' hearts so tightly weaved,

That the Conservatives of Westminster with their slim majority rule

Will be cautious in diplomacy or be made to look the fool.

With our countries' politics so different strong views will be expressed

So we can only ask, as we would ourselves, they do their very best,

They know failure's not an option and that the pressure will be felt

But I'm sure the guys will raise their voice and get Westminster telt!

The Doors are Locked.

To all those in Scotland who chose to vote No

Are you happy with what you achieved?

This is real life, it's sickening and it's your chosen show

I bet now you wish you believed.

All for a Union and all for a queen

This woman has caused all the fuss

But when you're sanctioned and starving, who're the ones to be seen

It won't be your queen, it'll be us!

At the door of compassion they pushed their way through

Begging for something to eat

Hands rose up to meet them, I saw some of you,

Yes! You of the social elite

Their eyes looked so empty as they squirmed on the floor

Their life is what they contest

They reached out to you but you closed the door

Hiding is what you do best.

They 're locked out and helpless, no strength for a fight

But others are taking their place

These people are fighting for their human rights

It's your name that will be disgraced

For all social justice, for workers you said

You're standing for all that is good

But the poor who are here, could soon wind up dead

And all for a mouthful of food.

When god dealt your cards, I bet your heart sank

Did you throw some and ask for a twist?

Where in this world of love do you rank

Since compassion is not on your list?

Did you feel all the sorrow and sadness you brought

Again and again and again

When that child is yours, you give without thought

You can't bear it for them to feel pain.

Your tyrannical speeches appease all your leeches

But you can't fool the fools all the time

They won't take a lecture from some rich tax inspector

A man made a Peer for his crimes

Can you really defend those who pretend

They're working for one and for all

There are no more closed doors, your road's a dead end

The people are now making the calls.

Amy Black.

As scripted friendships blossom

Into something felt so proudly

The silence of the airwaves

Seem to shout our pride so loudly

For blessed was I to answer

As she took what life taught her

I took her words and held them

From a future favourite daughter,

Scottish hearts are safe within the young.

We find errors on life's highways

Then correct them with life's tools

And judge not by the years they own

As the sage can be the fool

But be humbled by her inner thoughts

Which mirror those her age

For the young have wakened consciences

Unlike that dying sage,

He wanders in the desert that he made.

She's all that Scotland stands for

And all she represents

And early years are telling me,

It's the system she resents

Whilst tidal thoughts flood her young mind

Of a world in need of change

She sees the silt set in on brains

Whose laws are deemed deranged,

He's drowning in his ever sifting sands.

The poor are both their subjects

But their aims are poles apart

One is draining life itself

Whilst she reaches out to hearts

And waltzing in her innocence

Is a symphony she hears

And each note a faithful promise

To the dreams she holds so dear,

She holds the baton tightly in her hand.

Her hand is reaching out to all

Who have fallen in the stream

But they're only shallow waters

And its tide won't stop her dreams

She looks at me with ripened mind

As if saying it's her duty

Smiling through forsaken thoughts

She shows Fintry's youthful beauty,

Thank you for the thoughts within your mind.

The 56.

Cameron acknowledged but expect some delays

The Smithical Vow is on hold

He nods in agreement when faced with the facts

Thinking Scotland will do as she's told

And whilst he considers some cunning wee plan

With his cohorts who think they know best

We've plans of our own and it's time to disown

A party that we'll put to rest.

We've stood to attention, obeyed all the rules

As our people are smacked in the face

They've had enough, we've all had enough

It's time to get out of this place.

This Kingdom United is now torn apart

The richest have drawn their line

Below stand the multitude asking for more

Above stand the righteous, divine.

They travelled to London, into Parliament Square

And gazed at the houses so grand

They were our voices, this their new home

And they'd fight for their people and land,

The big and the bold stood with young and old

They represent all that is right

And as journeyman, novice, stand side by side

Their story will be Scotland's plight.

Fifty six voices of women and men

Who've all been elected by you

Will obey all the rules put together by fools

And put forth your points of view,

They sit with the richest yet fight for the poor

Austerity's what they must end

And whilst part of the system, they've a right to be heard

They're here as the poorest's best friend.

Lindsay Jarrett.

She's had operations and she's tried every pill

A disease for which there's no cure

She now needs a wheelchair, she is terminally ill

But she's a heart that's both clean and pure

Her lungs and her liver cannot be repaired

The medicines are working no more

She's mothered five children but could not prepare

For the heartache that lay in store.

Do you see her a rebel, outwith your command

A woman, courageous and bold

Who took back her life to fight for her land

A story that has to be told

With her children awaiting her one final stand

Their young hearts cannot be consoled

But they're with their best friend and will be to the end

Each one of them shares the same soul.

She gets looks from a world that look in from outside

She knows what goes on in their minds

They don't see the courage or passion inside

Or the thoughts of what she'll leave behind

She thinks of her loved ones and how they'll survive

In a place where the wealth isn't shared

She wants Independence, she's fighting for change

She wants a country that cares.

In the blackest of mornings she set a slow pace

Her oxygen strapped to her back

By Edinburgh castle she climbed the rock face,

Down below the train showed its tracks

The ex Police Inspector held in her hands

A boost for her loved Yes Campaign

Her Yes banner looked grand, it went just as she'd planned

It was Lindsay's first Capital gain.

She sat rightly proud whilst addressing a crowd

In the place we call Freedom Square

I heard her message, it was clear, it was loud

My first rally and glad I was there

It was Hope over Fear against all things austere

And the Yes flags were still on display

Dressed in bold tartan gear she wowed everyone here

Carpe Diem, she seized the day.

That Ol' Time Religion.

Religion's building barriers when it used to take them down

And it's still the greatest cause of war fought on someone's holy ground

But colour plays its evil part where the good are always white

And the black religion's always bad, they always start the fight!

The men who represent a god execute those who are gay

Then these same men abuse young kids and throw that life away

Their disciples rape and pillage all done in some god's name

But the men who give that blessing are they not the ones to blame?

"Forgive me Father for I have sinned" says the holy Catholic priest

I molested some parishioners – I became that dirty beast

He's absolved behind a panelled wall where a jury cannot hear

Then wanders freely round his streets where his victims live in fear.

Afraid to say what's going on or their God will strike them down

And the dirty beasts still make their rounds and maybe in your town

These people who abuse the cloth should be thrown into jail

It's not their god but you my friends; it's the people they have failed!

One Day.

Play once more the freeman's rhyme, sing its song to me

And when I hear the clock that chimes, I'll know my liberty.

The song is not the words I hear nor chimes of rhythmic bell

But the chains that break within this heart, that frees me from this spell,

My heart is crying out in pain from the sorrow in my mind

But when this heart sings out to me, freedom I will find.

Only The Dead Go With The Flow.

Oh you, such weary shallow men

Who falter to your manse

You sharpen up your carbon sticks

Then script your cash advance.

You dream with ermine round your necks

In all your pomp and circumstance

But when our piper plays our tune

We'll define the dance.

Flee you scallies from these isles

You're trusted here no more

Sever all your ties with us

And leave these islands' shores

There's not a man who gives a damn

For the uncouth, undignified

You're just another tarnished servant here,

Your boat leaves with the tide.

Your laws are not the laws for us

You defy the Sailor's scrolls

Entrapment is your deadly game

And poisoned are your souls.

Your lines are spun with fine deceit

But tangled is your web

You may be running with the tide

But remember tides have ebbs.

We are your chorus of the night

We're the nightmare in your dreams

And as your river gushes forth

We are its thousand streams.

We're the force behind you

We're the nation's blood

And the dam we built, you rush against,

Beware the people's flood.

Jaffafest.

You march with your feet and your heads in the clouds

Keeping time with your flutes and your drums banging loud

As your big banners fly so ornately adorned

Your tunes hide the words of the people you scorn.

You welcome all faiths but will admit only one

That's the protestant unionists, Ulster's bloody sons

Who play songs of hatred to prove a love to your queen

Does Fenian blood matter or are they still obscene?

You've become social outcasts, Scots don't want you here

And your 5 per cent supremacy no longer holds our fear

In all of your finery you camouflage what we know

Your sectarian hatred shines in your bigotted show

You say that you listen but you only hear what you want

That you don't incite riots and will ignore all the taunts

But you're the ones taunting you're the curse of this land

Will it go peacefully or will it get out of hand?

Good old Glasgow Labour Council, who again rebuked their town

With them at least they're constant, they always let you down!

Look, Listen and Learn.

It's not what they say but, indeed, what they do not

Our liberty is theirs to seize and not just that of Scots

The devil's their conscience; some strange god, their soul

Where speech isn't free, it's infiltrated by moles.

With rallies increasing is our attendance a test

Where civilians speak out doing their civil best

Against a culture that's growing and whose only intent

Is to rule over the poorest with their rod of contempt.

It's apartheid, a culling and they know they're in control

And do this by killing, destroying, our poorest lost souls

It's a thirst that's insatiable and will never be quenched

It's their ticket of dreams and one that's deeply entrenched.

Fair. Right. And just! We will fight here for all

Say the Tories whilst dining in their banqueting halls

They lecture with ease – all agreed by the Crown

But for the dead, no remorse, no apology, no, not even a frown.

Rebel and you suffer, swim against them you'll drown

Speak out, you'll be silenced, obey you're put down

Who are these people whom we trust with our voice

Are they now corporations backed by The Bullingdon Boys?

I've listened to speakers and what troubles their minds

And through all their words their hearts strongly bind

They want rid of austerity, they show they want to care

That's the Right, Just and Fair, we should all want to share.

Are we a heartbeat responding to the fear that they feel

Their turmoil is constant which is so badly concealed

They're fraught with common frailties but rise above the blame

But when it's simple economics, austerity's their shame.

Hypocrisy's calling so just what do we believe?

I see nobody richer yet see many more grieve

Like a virus they fester, attacking the poor, the infirm

And the warnings we gave have now all been confirmed.

I'm lucky, I can get debt if times get hard or severe

But I know that some can't and their lives get more austere

I know some sleep rough, but worse, I know more will die

Destitute, freezing, will government now hear their cries?

The Stranger We Should Know.

And when the sunrise comes to greet

The lonely man who hasn't slept

The commoner looks to a secret place

He knows how much he wept,

Lying still, the lonely man,

Has at last an interested crowd

And the commoner looked into his heart

That was neither loud nor proud.

He asked where all the good folk were

When the man crawled to his death

And why they all avoided him

'til he'd taken his last breath.

A broken heart had killed this man

Just another someone dead

And no-one got to know his name

That's not the way they're bred.

Is it worse to sit and wonder

If your help could change their fate

Or is it worse to pray for a man who's dead?

By then it's all too late.

Treat others as we treat ourselves

Is that not some unwritten law

Unwritten by the ones who care

Who some deem slightly flawed,

But I see people with a heart

Who don't feel the need to write

A people who believe in good

Who do what they think is right.

They give because they want to

They help because they can

They're the ones we should aspire to

They are the common man.

The Dreamers.

Just another coffee and one more cigarette, lazing on a café chair

Where I can dream and put the world to rights and prove to myself I care

I see curios strolling down these streets, others lost in some debate

Defiance, rushing through their heads 'til they're in explosive state.

Our heads are just a myriad, a movement full of thought

A maze we all can walk through and see exactly what we've got

But what is it we're looking for, to progress this disturbed mind

We engage and talk within our heads and feel for those so blind.

They cannot see the hurt they've caused and refuse to take the blame

We shout and baulk 'til we are hoarse in this cruel mindful game

Another puff, another sip, who will listen to my pleas

A dreamer who knows dreams are false, will you listen to me please?

I'm trying in this head of mine to right some of your wrongs

I'm looking at this world go by, a place where this mind can't belong

And these passers-by, whom I don't know, stroll along without a care

And the crowds who throng the tables, double up on some friends' chairs.

They sip their coffee, have a cigarette, laugh and talk in some debate

But laughing at a time like this when my mind is in this state

Why can't they see the beggars beg or the box that's someone's bed

They're oblivious to all my thoughts and what's inside my head.

They're blissful in their ignorance, lost in their own wee happy world

Wrapped in self indulgence where abuse cannot be hurled

Or am I just that dreamer who wants to see a world of change

And sees those people ruling us as no more than deranged.

This is not just fantasy it's a reality I share

With the millions who are dreamers and the millions more who care.

The Man Who Knew It All.

Carmichael, Alastair Carmichael! He of Frenchgate fame

This self-proclaimed Lord of his Isles cannot hang his head in shame

"I know nothing!" – Shultz insists, as he buries head in hands

A conniver, who failed our trust, and betrayed the people of his land.

He disgraced our First Minister, through a memo that he leaked

But this concocted lie will bring him down, in the havoc that he's wreaked.

Denying on denial, he led us on his merry Frenchgate dance

And Willie Rennie, THE master clown, wants to give him a second chance!

The great train robbers got jailed for life but this guy could walk Scot free

For fraud and conspiring to disgrace the leader of the SNP

And shown contempt towards the vulnerable, for his position he abused

He wasted 1.4 million pounds which our starving could have used!

He should be sacked, he should be jailed, just another sleekit Scot

A dishonoured rogue, all for himself, the others, he forgot

But in Shetland, his electorate march, with placards screaming "Liar"

I hope they don't build a Viking ship and set the thing on fire.

For with him on board, that lump o' lard, that's all the fuel they need

The fatted pig has gorged his last, he's been fed enough through greed!

Now, the noble House of Commons the guts to terminate his post

Or will they act, "like fair minded men", and pretend it's all a ghost;

His electorate crowd funded and gained enough financial support

To defy Westminster's justice and see this man in court.

But who was in it with him, who helped cover up his tracks?

Has he scratched the judge's back or is it just the old pals act?

He offered his apologies but at most it was benign

Guilty! And he knew it! Yet still would not resign

Should we forget what power is and the way it is misplaced

Well, remember Orkney, Shetland and the man who was disgraced!

The New Landlords.

Only standing together, can we break all they uphold

They've many flaws that we can see with their greatest being gold,

It comes in many colours and comes from land and sea

But mostly it's a shade of red where the locals' blood runs free.

They instruct the media with their lies, the power that we read

All in the name of patriotism then tell us why we must succeed

A dictator here, a tyrant there, who are threats to world peace

Are replaced by their new landlords who are only there on lease.

Who are these people playing with lives, these gods, all self ordained

We count the soldiers as they die whilst they count their golden grains

And the brave returning soldier has, no work, no home, no place

He's just a number in their world of greed, just another hollow face.

They were just obeying orders, doing what our soldiers do

But they fought for their masters who said they fought for you

Too many wars, too many deaths, all that suffering and pain

Where each life, lost or living, was offered up in vain.

In that one single moment when everything is still

The silence, the numbing, they'll say it's all god's will

On a cross, is a helmet but there's no writing, no name

Just a deathly reminder in the new landlord's game.

Laptops and Phones.

The Scottish Sun, The Daily Mail and the renowned Scottish Express

All differ in their headlines from the Welsh and English press

But the truth was always out there and these papers we disowned

It was the day we beat the media with just a laptop and a phone.

We started our own media sites, thousands joined up each day

Our simple truths outweighed their lies and the dirty games they played

A Wee Ginger Dug called Bella shouted out from Scot2Scot

And our Resistance grew a pair of Wings to deliver all our thoughts.

We built up our own social feeds, we became the voice

The hierarchy of the movement thought we had no choice

Factions sprouted everywhere, the seeds of love were sewn

It's amazing what you can achieve with just a laptop and a phone.

A language lost to most of us was reborn throughout the land

The Gaelic tongue is thriving when once THEY had it banned

We also found our history, their distorted facts were overthrown

We done all this with laptops and some psychedelic phones.

All the big guns muscle power track us night and day

Determined that by stalking us, we couldn't have our say

But couldn't, wouldn't can't exist in the minds of those who're free

There's a million Scots with laptops, phones and they're all the same as me.

Do I sense a nervous silence hanging like a thousand eyes

Do I detect the pounding hearts of Facebook's feeble spies

Get a grip and get a life, make your life your own

Get your laptop up and running and get yourself a phone.

We're flying through the stratosphere, Scotland's been reborn

The Saltire, our St Andrew's Cross, flies from our Unicorn

We awoke the proudest nation, Westminster's myths were finally blown

We're an army sitting on our arse, armed with laptops and with phones.

Your Nemesis.

Are you the righteous, strong and bold,

Who never makes mistakes?

Are you justified in telling them

To take that road you take?

How many take their own path

How many do you know?

Are they the one's who're selfish

Who take no-one on tow

And if you saw them on the street

Would you stop and say hello

Or would you with your narrow mind

Tell them where to go?

Is he the one you want to scream at

Because of a point of view

Or is this man you love to hate

Reminding you of you.

The Truth Is Out There.

Entrenched in superstition, our minds are not our own

They lease our thoughts on freedom, we never think alone

We declare a war upon ourselves, a war that never ends

Where "they" wine and dine our frailties and tell us they're our friends.

While we banquet on our apathy in a lavish thoughtful feast

They laugh behind their lying eyes and release the corporate beast,

They've been feeding us for centuries and always we obey

Their thoughts inflicted in our minds, forever leading us astray.

Have we lost the will to learn the truth and succumb to

what we're told

But once we analyse these tales, we see the truths unfold

Yet our history's being rewritten as we infiltrate their lies

Where they were rogues not heroes, just how much are they despised?

These writers dedicate their lives to what's already in our minds

They write because the truth is there, and those truths they will find.

Aye, Write!

They cower and cry, swathed in sweat, yet they cannot understand

As it feeds upon their feeblest minds, they bury heads in hands

Demoralised by this toxic waste it crawls inside their heads

And so afraid to face their children, they prefer the solace of their beds

This epidemic leaves them helpless as tears fall from their eyes

The suffering, we cannot see, and just how much they're demonised

It stays and preys within their minds, they face their greatest fear,

They lie confused and helpless, is their Armageddon here?

Their demons never give an inch; what have they now become?

Once they believed they wrote the truth and like addicts they succumbed

But the hacks attack with poisoned pens and conjure deadly deeds

And these rags that paralyse beliefs are led by venomous corporate greed.

This world of lies is killing them but there's an antidote to hand

We need controlled impartial writing, from the people of this land.

Ethnic Cleansing?

The highlands are empty, the glens are asleep

They forced out the families and replaced them with sheep

Some were killed by the pistol, some run through in steel

Killed, burned and butchered which the system concealed.

They were exiled to the corners of strange foreign shores

Forced out by the men who they fought for in wars

A lost Gaelic culture but at whose expense,

Was it the greed of the gentry or were we ethnically cleansed?

Crimea came calling and young Campbell was asked

Bring your chieftains, your clansmen, all you can amass

But he turned to his Lordship (whose loyalty's cheap)

You'll get no men here, you'd best arm your sheep.

The highlands are empty, the highlands are clear

We shipped out our fighters, they became pioneers

But when Britain came calling, they picked up their arms

And reminded old masters of some of their charms.

They fought for their freedom and fought with Scottish fight

They were Scotland's expelled given no bloody rights

Burned, tortured, maimed with their dead left behind

Now the gentry's own army against them were lined.

No chieftains, no clansmen, the hills were so bare

But tears from afar said they wished they were there

Once they were many but now they are few

And these losses, your Lordships, are all down to you.

You brought in your sheep to bolster your wealth

And cared not for the people, their culture or health

And the ramifications are still being felt

Death and destruction are what your deeds dealt.

Move On.

The mocking propagandists

Staged yet another tragic play

Then scorned with ease and detriment

At the proceeds of the day.

It was a sermon preached with fervour

From the pulpit of contempt

With the inclusiveness of madness

Which he savours with intent.

He delivered his emphatic speech

Which was met with great applause

From those who blocked amendments

To every single Scottish clause.

Our hopeful thoughts are in disarray

There is no comfort in despair

The barren band were roundly crushed

And those bleeding hearts, we share.

We were shown how to split the great divide

How to disunite a kingdom

He played his role impeccably

Is he the system or a symptom?

Yet beyond the words he finds with ease

Is a world against his will

And while the future world evolves

His will always be so still.

Abandonment.

Repercussions had to follow, they had to seek revenge

The atrocities, the slaughter, was theirs now to avenge

And when all this fighting's over, how do you treat your own

These heroes you once lauded, sleep in hovels all alone.

They're abandoned in a doorway, with their memories of war

Where a blanket and a begging bowl reminds them what they were
fighting for

Some lie awake in wheelchairs staring where limbs used to be

Blown away for their beliefs in today's democracy.

But if they deserted you just shot them, in their young backs as they fled

Or you lined them up and killed them with a bullet in the head

But it's you who are deserters; their blood is on your hands

You've abandoned those who fought for you when they terrorised those
lands.

There are countries you invaded and ones you will not leave

Is it for your love of killing or do you love to see them grieve?

Young children die of hunger, alone outside their home

As its rubble hides their parents, tell me, what have we become?

What is happening in this world and our love for fellow man,

Is extinction what you're after in these Middle Eastern lands?

There were no nuclear bases but promises were made

To the moguls you made deals with, did wealth make you invade?

These cities once so beautiful lie amongst the desert dust

And the unexploded bombs you sent, lie just gathering rust

But the innocents remember, this was all a war on want

And now the deaths they live with have all come back to haunt.

You're not bloodless, you're the killers, you signed the dotted line

Then protested you were justified as gold flowed through your mind

You thought of all the wealth you'd have, that's how much you care

And the insurgents that you vilified were just protecting what was theirs.

The world of yours is make believe where nothing's as it seems

I'd love to get inside your heads and trace your wildest dreams

But I'd only find a puppet controlled by our western banks

Whose fundraisers are soldiers who make you money with our tanks!

OXI.

When the weight of all you've ever known comes crashing to the ground

And you look for help from all your friends but no help's to be found

When the majesty of family, desert your every need

Your acquaintance is but rivalry to their more fashionable greed.

Masquerading as some worthwhile gods behind a painted smile,

Your acceptance to democracy shows a continent so vile

Use the system, flout the rules but mostly know its flaws

Your time in this democracy depends on loopholes in their laws.

It's an almanac of slavery that engulfs the world you crave

This nor any other lands, fights for the free and brave

The founding father of democracy left us a legacy of pride

But these European democrats are no more than bankers' brides.

They're the reason for this crisis as they play god with Greek lives

They can demolish all the temples but Greece will still survive

This nation's been bailed out before and will likely be again

By banks and bankers, so corrupt, with the natives, once more, slain.

There's the sound of German jackboots marching with some old salute

And following like cackling geese are the SS dressed in suits

They could have taken guns or knives or bombed them with their tanks

But complete and utter desolation is only dealt through banks.

Bring your country's assets as collateral for bail

While they rain down more austerity to ensure that Greece will fail

They've shown contempt, disrespect, and proved they do not care

They spurned not just one nation but nations everywhere.

Their worthless words condemns mankind as nations sheds their tears

They're the devil's compromise of death and all austere

They're the ones who sharpen knives and polish coldest steel

They're the ones who'll slit your throat then ask you how you feel

They're your lords and masters and with our lives they play

They empower us with useless words, we do not have a say.

They're the ones who shout unite but divide with every chance

They're the ones who call the tune and we're the mugs who dance

They're sacrosanct within this sect, the untouchables in law

But one country stood against them, OXI equals Naw!

My Name's Tim and I'm a Born Leader.

Tim, a simple question, is gay sex right or wrong

He stutters out his answers but his answers don't belong

Quoting from his good book he avoids it yet again

As the interviewer asks: Should men have sex with men?

He says his views are Liberal and for the benefit of all

But when he's asked a question, he falters thrice then stalls

Yet he's quick to condemn half of Scots who supported SNP

We're arrogant, authoritarian, we're the Big Brother entity!

We're insurgents in ascendancy where insanity's taken hold

Mr Farron, we're right minded, sane and proud and bold

Right for standing up to you and all your cronies in the halls

Our party's a minority but at least they've got the balls

To fight against the tyranny whose views were voiced by you

Your words are worse than meaningless so keep your points of view

You sat with them on Question time yet you never said a word

But now you hide behind the media whose bias is absurd

You know you sound just like a Nazi from a different bygone age

But your anger's aimed at something else in another wayward rage

Is it Frenchgate or Carmichael, is it retribution at all costs

You lied to your constituents, that's the reason that you lost!

Or do you think you're some Messiah come to settle one last score

You're the same as all the rest of them, like the preachers here before.

Get Tae!

You listened intently then applauded so gently

As blue blood now runs through your veins

You turned your backs to the wall when the SNP called

Now there's nothing more left to explain.

You won't help the workers, you've scorned the poor

Can you tell me why you even exist?

You are meant to repel, this austerity hell

But that help for the poor you dismissed!

You dug deep your trenches, then deserted your benches

Were you embarrassed, guilty or both

But the bold SNP took your seats that were free

At least someone's still keeping their oath.

It was a sign of defiance as they sought your alliance

To fight for what they know what is right

But you haven't the gall, you've not even got Balls

You're just a rabble that's riddled with spite.

There was Hardie and Benn, proper socialist men

But then came Blair and then Brown

You're meant to contest, this one holy mess

But like the latter, abandoned your ground.

You've chosen the path that deals only in wrath

From a party you've joined at the hip

But the word from ex voters, now think you are stoatirs

You're the ones who abandoned your ship!

Life, Love and Hate.

We've to learn to love but our great gods above

Are ensuring we know how to hate

The doctrines they preach have all but been breached

We're just listening too much to the state.

We've to live by their rules that divide us by schools

In their religious divisional corps

These sweet benefactors are nothing but actors

And this world is their stage, nothing more.

Whether black, white or brown, we cannot be found

To judge by the colour of skin

Babies don't know their race or their colour of face

'Til the hate from the adults sets in.

They teach us to embrace but their deeds are disgraced

Our tutors are nothing but masks

For some life is sacred for others it's hatred

For others you'll just have to ask.

Our time here is measured by laughter we've treasured

And to bury those things we regret

But the friendships we find are forever in mind,

Special times we can never forget.

The Thin White Line.

His stare is cold his eyes are dark but he's a friend that hits the mark

And takes it with him everywhere he goes

His long hard hours are in disguise, a sparkle now fills once black eyes

As the line of powder's hoovered up his nose.

This common man is being adored by commoners and sometimes lords

And occasionally the ladies choose

To help themselves to thin white lines and leave their troubles all behind

In corridors where MPs share the loos.

On hairdryers and toilet bowls, these powder rooms in power halls

Seem to be the places to abuse

So if you see a brown nose on the ground who knows what they're sniffing round

As substantial noses know how much to use.

So if you see your MPs taking fright or hear them talking utter shite

It could be that wee line up their nose.

It helps them in their time of need and soon they'll have another feed

As another pair of nostrils gets a doze.

The working man is ostracised but the elitists think it Paradise

Before the sacrificial altar gets a swab

What's good for them is good for me say all the other straight Mps

But all they get is just a sherbet dab!

A Past For A Future.

With his clansmen he enters, all men who were there

Their ghosts, a reminder, of a proud race who dared

They come in the night time, all of them, strangers to me

Only clansmen exclaiming, we need to be free.

They lean on their broadswords, stand behind shields

Brave and alert and unwilling to yield

They died at Culloden then rose from their fall

They're recruiting and hoping, Scotland answers their calls.

A gentle voice whispers but the words are sincere

Their fight's for the freedom of a land they hold dear

They stay for a while but then say they must go

I ask where they're going but I already know.

They're going back to Culloden to relive liberty's fight

Licking blood from the wounds that they clean every night

But their nightly returns only bring more sorrow and pain

Then say the Scotland I love will be free once again.

I saw men slain in battle, young sons by their side

Their liberty ended but their deaths carried pride

Let those from the present stand up to their past

And may the voice of those people be heard here at last.

From Sea to Shore.

He searched and searched to find his kind but there was no-one left behind,

So he preyed upon himself within his mind

His mind confused at being abused, his honest people felt accused

Their daily lives were now so much maligned

But those destitute were resolute and knew their acts would be rebuked

As he wiped the tears from his embittered face

The old man's from another place, a time when moral laws disgraced

Which history itself will not embrace.

He looked at those which life denied and then at mourners as they cried

But their overlords and masters were not crying

The old man knew this was the end, as the factors laughed and scorned his friends

Who said they were no good but good at dying.

And sitting in that lonely place another tear another face

His cards, they could have dealt a little kinder

And as the old man looked along, he sung out loud the crofters' song

But his masters just looked on, a sharp reminder.

He remembered when he saw first saw this land and stretches of its golden sand

When he himself and others were the strangers

But the old land lived within his head where he rejected all the factors said

So far away but now he faced new dangers.

Animals now roamed his land, it's what his lords had neatly planned

Ejected from the only life he knew

First shipped to sea then shipped to shore, the old land he would see no more

As the gun and fire masters quickly slew.

Some were drowned in ships at sea, others made it just like me

But death, they said, was their preferred option

Dead they were inside their heads for in their places sheep were led

And on a coast somewhere signed papers of adoption

One day we'll see our hills and glens, the highlands will be ours again

But in his heart he knew it was too late

There are no crofters left today, the sea has swept them all away

Their lords and masters made sure of their fate.

But some memories are never told and how the factors killed for gold

As another mother's home was set ablaze

They locked the families deep inside, three generations burned alive

The Clearances, their ethnic cleansing days

But teachers don't teach this at school, they're governed by the factor's rules

Your history has always been distorted

It's written by those holding power, it's theirs alone and never ours

The writings must reflect but be contorted.

They lied about our history and lied about our slavery

They won't face up to who they really are

History is from the past with ancient memories meant to last

But what we learn leaves us badly scarred

We're finding more and more each day that remind us of the games they play

We're living in a prison ruled by jailers

I asked this question they replied by asking me: Well, who am I?

So I answered them, an old man and a sailor

I'm that old man, the crofter and a sailor.

I was a crofter once but now a sailor.

My Name is Lord Sewel.

He's no spring chicken, sixty nine, his sex and drugs keep him in line

This self confessed animal loves a party

Another flat in Dolphin Square and an ex comrade of Tony Blair

No wonder he wants to be led astray

Two ladies came unto his door, each one undressed and each a whore

Two hundred pounds a night their separate fees

In super pomp and super pose, a banknote hung from this Lord's nose

Dangling there for all the world to see

His lines of coke lined up the girls and snorted 'til his mind had birled

This minister knew just what he was after

I'm sure that he enjoyed his ride and rightfully was criticised

As the sordid air was now filled with their laughter

An expensive night I hear you say, I hope he got his wicked way

Please remember we pay his expenses

If I'd a grand a night to spare, I'd make sure I'd no cameras there

And maybe enjoy more my recompenses

A kind man, gem, an utter jewel, a titled man, his name Lord Sewel

His House of Lords job now looks in tatters

A deputy addressing Lords before going on to undress whores

Two ladies, who would his ego, flatter

I suppose a Lord when paying for whores should not take snapshots by a door

Disloyalty is just a click away

If the oldest trade is prostitution then right behind is retribution

Never picture Lords whilst they're at play

Your camera can be friend or foe, I would have said but you now know

And did we, the public, pay them for his favours

They sign a declaration code but now do they sign in naked mode

This man uphold their standards of behaviour

The Lords are seen a bloody joke and not just for their lines of coke

The unelected chosen for donations

Their lives are judged on their lifestyles, the prostitutes, the paedophiles

He's one less worry, one more resignation.

Just Another Peer.

There's a lady in waiting, one Michelle Mone

Just another wee sheep who's about to be cloned

They'll be running around with their bleats and their baas

All dressed up in fine ermine wearing Ultimo bras.

Like the one advertised by Lord Sewel in the Sun

Just before Rupert Murdoch got the poor bastard done

But if Mone could make condoms, her share prices would soar

For the pricks that she sits with are all bloody whores.

Michelle, you deserve this, a titled lady at last

But is it a step up from your names in the past?

From a lingerie queen to illegitimate peer

You'll soon be at one with the rest of the queers

Just how many rogues are in this parcel of shame

Too many to mention and all without blame.

Dolphin House.

(Allegedly - so they tell me).

In the land of the living

The dead walk the streets

With visions of you in their mind

They want you Ted Heath

All you left was a wreath

Around a headstone, they carry, unsigned

They're just looking for justice

They don't want revenge

They felt not your pleasure but pain

You took life from the living

Blackened their souls

Then fucked up their bodies and brains.

Depraved and neglected

Orphaned, denied,

They screamed but no-one was there

With no-one in the hall

They could not hear your call

And all the rooms were too busy to hear

Now tortured minds wander

Beside crippled hearts

As the media turns its blind eye

They talk about Policing

And speak of the costs

Never speaking of those who had died.

Did the conscierge know

About their little side shows

In their games of sexual pursuits

Or did the brave little bastards

Succumb to their masters

The Satanists dressed up in suits

From London to Jersey

From Wiltshire to Kent

Police forces are sifting through files

Rotten right to the core

I ask, how many more

Are earning from these paedophiles.

What of Jill Dando,

Our own Willie MacRae,

They were both shot through the head

And what of the criminals

What of their crimes

They're only found guilty when dead.

They're either thrown out court

Or the law just aborts

Saying well done, you're now free to go

We know it's all lies

We know more will die

Welcome to The Westminster Show.

Fool's Gold.

Don't blame the poor, the homeless, the sick, underpaid

They're the systematic victims who don't make the bankers' grade

But they're essential to their corporate world where every penny counts

For they see the poor as golden bars and each one a weighty ounce

It's they who are the scavengers and it's they who make the rules

And our poor are just necessities but viewed as necessary fools

They're ruthless masters of the finance game and know each bill that's passed

Is helped on by our government whose own personal wealth's amassed

We have Gideon, an expert, who's always there to lend a hand

A failed economic expert but their will is his command

He's the ultimate disaster, the village idiot in his school

And probably bullied every day, but plainly, still a fool

But he's a fool whose worth is millions, a man who plays their game

He's a cog within a system where no-one rich gets blamed

So don't blame the poor, the homeless, the sick, the underpaid

They're the systematic victims who don't make the bankers' grade.

A Date in Freedom Square.

When will Glasgow's Labour Council do as the people want

Instead of going against them with their never ending taunts

We are many

They are few

I will walk

Will you?

Will you march on Freedom Square with Saltires flying high

And will we see your faces there or will we be denied?

Will you show hope can conquer fear, is it time to seize the day?

It was Scotland's voice and Scotland's choice, to stay or break away.

But tell me who you really are and who you want to be

Your soul is crying out to you, is it your choice to set it free?

We spoke as one in May this year when we all stood side by side

When we went with our Hopes and voted with our Scottish pride.

This is our referendum's anniversary and we will stand again

Side by side and singing out with families and friends

Thousands out there jumping, alive in freedom Square

And of the thousands dancing, will your face be there?

All Hail The Dug!

Oh! The choices life throws at us and we're expected to be right

But if it's a vote for Labour's leader, now that's a different fight.

They've had a few, all pretty sad, but they'd still to make a choice

But take the last one and the runner-up, would you lend them your voice?

The bold Murphy saw a pair of legs but could not find a brain

And Queen Kezia was just like him and one he called his ain

She took comfort in his Irn Bru and they often shared a slug

So he became the master and she, his charming Dug.

And so they travelled far and wide, skipping, linking arms

It never takes a lot to sway a woman with her charms

She's particular in who she sides with, but, seemingly not in bed

For she's just another Torylight, the type who's coloured red.

Her and Fundily Mundily would have made the perfect pair

Him upon his plastic crate, screaming lies at every square

Attacking was their forte and he loved showing his physique

And never knew if he'd won or lost 'til told by his media clique

And she, the swooning damsel, she of the snarling face

Both sneering at their public and being publicly disgraced.

You can't humiliate the brainless when all they have are glaikit smiles

And yet both think they'll rule Scotland from Edinburgh's Royal Mile

You see Jim has got a juggling spot and The Dug's his pretty aide

Will this be Labour's new HQ, where their policies are made?

At least they'll have an audience, a new lot from the fringe

Another crowd, another breed, another lot who'll cringe

But now she's their new gaffer, will they rise up and be strong

Or will we show them one more time, where they all belong?

Even Corbyn cannot save them with his outspoken leftist views

A man who came to Scotland and captured headline news

Who spoke of England's southern lands right up to Carlisle

But had no answers/questions from Kezia's Royal Mile.

He went against her nuclear wars and will refuse her further powers

And cancelled out an Indy 2 when that choice alone is ours,

He fell at every obstacle but I'm sure he'll sway The Dug

Just a brainless little lady but still the same old mug.

Both charismatic secretaries, a trait they seem to own

Just put a collar round her neck with a kennel for her throne.

It's a shame political weddings are not ours to promote

For if Glaikitness could ever wed, they would get my vote.

Glamis, Bowes-Lyon and The Unicorn.

(Written after a visit to Glamis Castle on 8th August 2015).

Its driveway is magnificent with its manicured lush lawns

A cultured highland entrance with sculpted centuries of dawns

Its tended trees line the narrow drive that sweeps into the night

But at the other end, there lies, Glamis Castle's wondrous sight.

It's like a fairy tale, quaint and pretty and is completely tartan free

Which seemed so out of character for an estate outside Dundee

Whilst its armoury and armaments hung from every wall I saw

It was the unicorns, pre Union years, that left this man in awe.

Scriptures hung and plaques portrayed a Unicorn standing free,

Not bound in harshest golden chains, a symbol of our liberty

Hanging portraits adorn ancient walls with links to ancient crowns

But as we toured the cold stone rooms, I think they thought us clowns!

To commemorate our "Union's" birth a heraldic plaque was cast

But to me this plaque, 1603, hides a dark and sordid past

My fascination with the Unicorn led my eyes to see

That this proud and wild Scottish beast, was here, no longer free

I asked the question to myself, what are they trying to hide?

And so strange was this anomaly I begged the question to my guide

But she'd never seen the beast in chains and scorned the term "oppressed"

Had we sold our souls for chains of gold and were we now possessed?

Tied and bound, he could not move, he was trapped in golden chains

Yet before, he'd always been so free, but now this Union reigned.

But it depicted to me sadness when I realised that fateful date

1603, our Union's birth, was when Scots were filled with hate

Battles raged and blood ran free in every city, village, town

They rebelled against a Union and dismissed the joint crowns.

The common Englishman didn't want it, nor did the common Scot

But our history's underwritten and lies are what we're taught.

Which other country worldwide would deny the citizens their right

To fly their country's Saltire flag incase it starts a fight!

This Union sees us rebels, when all I see are men

Men who ask for civil rights but are put down once again

Bowes Lyon and their stately Glamis, a castle of past times

Its walls run deep and stained with blood, it's where they hid their royal crimes.

I asked about the madness, how the queen mother gained the throne

But the answers came from staring eyes, "best leave well all alone".

I hear you scorn and laugh at me but chains were never there before

So answer me my questions or scorn my words no more!

For Peace of Mind.

We were borne out of love and it's love we should give

These killings must stop and let people live

For drugs, oil, gold, foreign lands we invade

Then leave children as orphans hanging over a spade

As they crawl through the rubble to a life they can't save

They dig through their tears beside the mass graves.

 In Iraq and in Libya they were killed for black gold

And Afghanistan's drugs sales have increased since tenfold

They weren't a threat but we were sent in to kill

For the love of a pound or a crisp dollar bill.

They say it's for peace as if these deeds are kind

As Israelis continue killings and bombing Palestine

They'll rob you of your dollars then charge interest in pounds

Their culture is money, that's their common ground

Their chalice is poisoned and full to the brim

But they point to the soldier and blame it on him

There he lies buried below some god's earth

By a cross, disc and number, was that all he was worth?

The Betrayal and Death of William Wallace.

The pact was signed in Rutherglen's Kirk where a name would be revealed

Just another Scotsman's life betrayed, another Scot whose fate was sealed

He was captured at Robroyston by a sheriff cried Menteith

And would see no more his Scotland nor Scotland's air he'd breathe.

In silence they dispatched the news, their riders swiftly raced

To alert King Edward Longshanks, that The Wallace was disgraced

For three long weeks, bound hands and feet, they paraded England's prize

Though anger raged within his heart, a sadness filled his eyes.

The farcical trial, by a "foreign" court, was held at Westminster Hall

He would not bow down to England's crown nor to their cabal

So the pre-determined verdict claimed that a "traitor's" death he'd face

And at Smithfield's Haberdasher's Hall, the gallows took their place.

Chained naked to a wooden frame, he was dragged o'er the cobbled stones

He was pelted by what came to hand as their King took to his royal throne

Wallace laid his brutal body bare, ravaged by the entertainment of the day

He faced his death, his time was now, not another word he'd say.

Hanged then dropped whilst still alive, the rope jerked his body tight

Then in full view cut his privy parts and burned them within his sight

His stomach slit then disembowelled and his entrails shown to the crowd

Then thrown into the brazier as the executioner had avowed.

The hangman held his knife aloft then opened up his chest,

And pulled out the warm and beating heart, a skill the hangman must possess

Then cut off his head and held it high for all the crowd to see

Then quartered up his body parts, all done by Royal decree.

His limbs were sent to Newcastle, Berwick, Stirling and Perth,

The sentence for a Scottish knight who committed treason on his earth

Wallace's head was spiked on Tower Bridge to embarrass Scotland's son

And to put the fear of Christ in Scots but this was all to be undone.

A barbaric death in barbaric times but it was a death held back for Scots

This was the devil's work, pure butchery, another evil Royal plot

But tales of William Wallace spread and a martyr he became

And far beyond this island's realms Freedom claimed the Wallace name.

When a man stands up for his beliefs and stands up for what is right

There is no power can match the human faith, not even Royal might

Wallace lives in us today, in the heart of every Scot

But his Freedom is a right for all and not what we've been taught.

The Talking Dug.

Each summer all the kids go mad when the circus comes to town

But we've got one that's stayed behind and they're with us all year round

It's called The Labour Party but it's just its Scottish Branch

But they're just a bunch of cowboys and it's a Dug that runs the ranch.

They've clowns galore, comedians and put on some special shows

And it's free to watch their no holds barred, here, anything goes

They say they're talking politics but we know that's all just bull

I mean, they've got a Dug that talks, yet they call us the fools

She cracks the jokes and gets the laughs I wish I wrote her scripts

But this Dug keeps stitching arseholes cos each day a new one's ripped

Most her gags are just ad-lib and they get the best applause

And I'm sure her walkers just agree, or they'll feel her biting jaws

The Dug runs round unleashed, unchained, like a terrier on speed

Snapping, yelping, running mad like some lost demented breed

Her poor dad always slags her off but that just adds to her charm

But he needn't have said anything; she's an expert at self harm

Well, that's the Dug and what she says is not always what you hear

Maybe she'd be better off, listening to, her father dear.

The Cost of Benefits.

His eagerness is never swayed and he never makes mistakes

His sniping up an east end close, one shot is all it takes

This psychopathic killer treads his own psychopathic path

This marksman doesn't need a gun just co-operative staff.

He forces staff to contravene some of our basic human rights

Forcing sanctions on their neighbours who're left helpless in their plight

But the subtle knife of Mr Smith is twisted like his tongue

He's a dark heart with unconscious soul, destruction's all he's brung.

He won't do confrontation and any blame is just denied

He stands by his fabricated tales and all truths he'll cast aside

He thinks death insignificant and is not afraid to say

They're just another dying nobody, he doesn't have to pay.

Your successful claims are blatant lies, to which you, yourself confessed

Whilst claimants in the real world reach your targets with their deaths

You even sanctioned those who're dead, is nothing sacrosanct

But by saving all this money, deaths are all you've banked.

You call them scroungers cheats and liars yet force them into debt

Poverty is all they have, and from you, that's all they'll get

You don't care if you break the rules or how many laws you've breached

And care not who survives or dies, your target must be reached.

Different Cast Same Script.

They're determined to crush us in our search to be free

But none are determined, as determined as we

We are ably backed by our street volunteers

Not marching with guns or a strapped bandolier

They march with their feet and are guided by hearts

That want a new Scotland and a bright brand new start

But if just one should resist or fail in their plight

There are a thousand more waiting to take up the fight

They're not marching for money but for country and pride

A pride the establishment, try their utmost to hide

They don't run this country, they control, they demand

They just do what they like "for what's best for these lands"

It's what's good for their pockets, their profits, their shares

Their rich royal connections and their rich royal heirs

They fear for their mansions, their lands and their gold

They've the blackest of hearts and the blackest of souls

These elected providers fail the poor every day

Like an old film we sit through it and watch the replays

Every movement rehearsed, every act carefully planned

A different cast recites the words by the same old crooked hand.

The Kennel Club.

The Dug's called for a reunion of members present, past

And hired the local café for the crowds that might amass

Magrit couldnae make it, she says she's had enough

And far too busy signing on yet still looking just as gruff

In a coat that's hanging back to front, this one's buttoned up the side

While her mate is doing all he can, to promote his Park and Ride Yep,

Matheson's found another car, well, that's another arse being felt

While Wee Jola's struggling on in life and admits that she got telt

The Buddies showed wee Dougie that Paisley's still got style

And made it clear to Alexander that he is Nobody's Child

And Fundilly's got his own TV show, Sunday Sermons From A Crate

It seems as though his paradise has come a bit too late

But he was always late and second rate, and completely out of touch

I miss the anger, blatant lies, he gave us oh! so much.

The Shadows.

(The ones who went missing at the final hurdle).

They followed your wisdom

They believed you were right

They accepted your dreams

And gave you their fight

But where did you go to

In their hour of need

Back in the shadows

Where you hid with your greed.

You were afraid of commitment

Yet you were their choice

But you became their denial

You denied them your voice

You stepped into your shadow

You don't want to be seen

And while they seek their leader

You call them obscene.

They would have stood by you

You had their conviction

But you let them hang

In their own crucifixion

You watched them die

You drove nails in their cross

Words have no meaning

When honour is lost.

How could you betray them

They knocked on your door

You professed your allegiance

Their allegiance they swore

But as the day grew nearer

Fate dealt a blackened hand

You retreated to your shadows

And lost your Independent land.

Culloden's Red Skies.

While some fought for religion or fought for a crown

Some gave up their sons for their own hallowed ground

But none revered the coward or the coward's selfish act

And none felt for the father when he signed his evil pact.

Would you forfeit your sons for the sake of your land

Would you sign their death warrants with your honest hand

Would you send one, a rebel, for the Jacobite cause

To oppose his own brother and protect all your flaws?

As they faced each other with their father's steel swords

Which one would fall, the Laird's or the Lord's

He was willing to pay for a lifestyle so grand

With the death of a son by the other son's hand!

Some fought for their freedom, some fought for a crown

And here they lie dead on a blood sodden ground

Culloden's still crying at a war that was won

When brother fought brother and father killed son.

On the field of the killings the sky was turned red

Reflecting the blood of all sons lying dead

Their ghosts look for loved ones with tears in their eyes

As their deaths are reflected in Culloden's red skies.

The sun sets on secrets but are awakened at dawn

When the truth comes to light that his sons were but pawns

He betrayed his own sons for the sake of some land

He slew his sons with that cowardly hand.

He had no sense of honour, pride or dignity

A man whose guilt will never set him free

But many more were like him and, sadly, many more still are,

They all bring in the riches with no sign of battle scars.

Loud and Proud.

I've been on this journey three short years

A much shorter time than some

But I've travelled back through centuries

To find what we've become

I've walked with you when far away

And wrote down with this pen

Words that came from all of you

Time and time again.

Like pilgrims on their holy walk

You sought like souls possessed

That Holy Grail within your heart

You thought was repossessed

You believed your country

Should be free from being oppressed

And from that belief an army rose

This movement known as Yes.

Independence was your vision

Liberty your aim

And through your dedication

Scotland was reclaimed

The strength that lies within you

The power that you hold

Is the richest gift you'll ever have

More precious than their gold

Defeat has made us stronger

And divided, must not be

We must be strong and take our chance

The chance that makes us free

To be independent of a government

That constant thorn in our side

That London centric stronghold

That takes us for a ride

I've seen heroes, martyrs, our ancestral rights

Die on every page

I've wept tears of pride and sadness

But always felt engaged

How proud I was to chart your rise

Yes, you lot make me proud

And when I say I thank you

I say that loud and proud.

We will be the victors soon

Of that I have no doubt

And when our independence comes

We'll see the Tories out.

The Choirmasters.

We're a chorus of critics, that's all, just a choir

Where we stand and what we sing as their baton rises higher

They've orchestrated every word and though the chorus may be ours

It's the verses that they keep from us that hide controlling powers.

Don't let them hold the baton, refuse to sing along

Listen to what's in your heart and let that be your song

A verse is an agenda and handpicked only by the few

They judge you on its content then hold judgement when you're through.

Free means it's for nothing but nothing here is free

You'll pay a lifetime over and they'll still own your liberty

Hard work counts for nothing; they'll always pull the strings

But if we sing our own song who knows what that will bring?

All this online slagging, you play into their hands

As you trade your petty insults you just follow their demands

If something's worthwhile having then prepare with all your might

Is the freedom of your country not worthy of your fight?

Questions?

Do you wear a mask

When you fly your plane

Do you paint your face

Do you change your name?

Can I come with you

Will you let me fly

I want to see

How our enemies die

Are you told to go

Do you volunteer

And when you've bombed

Do you shout and cheer?

Why do you go

When you could end up dead

Or do you bomb

Like the protestors said

Do you drop your bombs

On the poor instead

They can't fight back………………………YOU CAN'T BE DEAD!

What Goes On Tour, Goes Down Here!

Westminster, who love us, are failing to show they inspire

And if I stand against them do my theories lend to conspire

Will they throw me in jail for tending to call them a liar

Or if we don't fly the Unionist flag but fly our Saltires?

"Wheesht"! said young Michael, The Cooncil can't know that we're here

Aye! Right! When two hundred bikers are hitting top gear

They rode round The Square to the cheers from Hope over Fear

Then revved to a level that might waken up Labour's peers!

All the people said Aye! When the council wanted us banned

And a lassie said Aye! When her boyfriend asked for her hand

Then The Boys fae the Scheme, The Twa Tenors, sang them a song

And we all joined in and told them, here's where they belong.

Denise in a kilt held her placard on a monument high

It had a blue and white Saltire, worded, that said she was Aye!

Amanda the chanter's wee daughter was there by her side

And like angels they looked on our Square that was bursting wi' pride.

Two Union flags flew but for them, they came a day late

Or was it on purpose, did they come here just out of hate?

If they'd come the right day, they could've joined that throng numbered eight

But our police saw them off and The Yes family thought it was great.

Fundily Mundily appeared on a beer bottle from our own Kay McCall

And that big glaikit face was screened and laughed at by all

He's a gift that keeps giving even though he's back in Transvaal

He will always be with us but now it's just on our pub crawls!

Some can't feed their kids but they're banning our school children's meals

If they want social cleansing I wish they'd stop dragging their heels

Try going without and tell me to my face how it feels

All this pain and the suffering, it's just another Tory ideal.

Do these rallies not show you that we'll be the ones to ascend

We are the ones on the rise not the ones who're condemned

Even Dugdale and Lamont have said they can no longer pretend

So we're sending Westminster to Hell with all of their friends.

Squealers!

As you unzipped your trousers did the film crew stand by your side?

Did they ogle then laugh as you held out your manhood with pride?

Did you look at the pig and wonder just how it would feel?

And were you more than surprised when the head of your pig didn't squeal?

Did you not realise that this pig was already dead?

It had no fucking body or did you have that before in your bed?

And did the thought of you waking beside it not fill you with dread?

You'll have us all thinking that all elitists are sick in the head!

Did you think of your future, I forgot, you cannot make plans

You just jump to attention when your masters make their commands

We now know your brains are not where they're supposed to be

But no doubt wee Lizzie will knight you for services to piggeries!

The animal Welfare Society will have a field day

Looking for Bullingdon Boys amongst all the pigs eating hay

While your children on field work shout "Father, what have you done"?

"Just watch your dear father, you're time is coming my son"!!!

They say we have choices but our media's fully controlled

They're on red alert to punish the Cybernat Trolls

But the ones they should watch are their donors, their billionaire friends

For pigs in a blanket can squeal if you care to offend!

Squealers. Part Deux.

It was only a prank, just a wee lost Bullingdon joke

This was no can of worms but a massive pig in a poke

When Dave goes to the butcher's for sausages does he insist on prime

But these posh boys' games that they play, are they animal crimes?

Was it Danish or Irish or Ayrshire or was it Halal

Or did he just close his eyes and think of his Tory best pal

If it was me he would say, how low can those poor people get

But this isn't about me, it's you, you frustrated vet!

When Miliband ate that ham sandwich did you see his wee face

Did he know something we didn't or are my thoughts misplaced?

Will bacon sales fall, will we all become veggies instead

What a graphic reminder of that wee dead pig's head.

The farmers are raging that sales on their pigs have gone down

But the heads sell for double to Bullingdon's perverted clowns

We all make mistakes but this time Davie's taking the hit

For it's him, no-one else, who's the proverbial pig in the shit!

Will they now shout Oink! Oink! Instead of Hear Hear in The Halls

Will Cameron quit or face up to the "Porky" type calls?

Oor Nicola and Alex were slagged for their fish sounding names

But it's Ham-fisted Davie who's The King of The Bestial games.

When Nothing Is Left.

Does this current Prime Minister listen to you and your views?

Does he talk for the nation at large, does he represent you?

Does he care for the workers; does he share your financial despair?

If you're old or you're poor, do you think he knows how to care?

They go to their "Etons" and are taught that one day they will rule

But just how much in common have we, with those types of schools?

These are people in mansions and butlers with money on tap

And their escorts are clicked by a finger to dance on their laps.

Debauchery rules but their antics are all washed away

They just sneer at the housemaids who clean up their mess every day

They're above any justice and destruction's all part of their game,

They think they're immune to our laws and refuse any blame.

Each follow a code so perverse, even then they're a team

All part of a pals' act they'll bring to their future regime

It's a system beyond us that only elitists can know

Where the rich and the royal engage, we're not part of their show!

We talk about Piggate and coke snorting toffs with their whores

We're talking of ministers walking through every closed door

They wine and they dine with caviar, finest champagnes

Then trash up the restaurant but know they'll get back in again.

Do you dine like this then act as though nothing is wrong?

Are they working class heroes, do you think that's where they belong?

I don't know the answer but I know better people than they

But they're out on the fringes and the media won't give them their say.

These elitists in power are up there and living a lie

Dressed in their finery, laughing, as poor people die

Look all around you; we're falling apart at the seams

All these wars and the killings are their money making machines.

Look at the countries, count up just how many have died

And look who invaded then tell me governments don't lie

We are covered in blood and wonder why those people flee

Before we went in, they were ruled, but at least they were free.

But their wars will continue, these Powerlords don't have our shame

And when nothing is left, remember: It was not done in my name.

They're Kings of their chessboard and the pawns are our submissive lives

And they look from their castle and don't care if we die or survive.

How many are lost every day in eternal war games

We live out their memories from staring at faces in frames

We might wear a poppy to remember those deaths in some war

Then sit back and wonder, what was their death really for?

Stop blaming each other, stop warring and start blaming them

It's they who are guilty and it's they who should be condemned

I'm sure if we're asked we would choose a world that's at peace

But as long as they are in power, the killings won't cease.

Our lives mean nothing, they'll relish the day when we're gone

And they'll tramp down the dirt that covers us, dusk until dawn

We're the victims of privileged lives and held in their fear

But the day we escape from their grip grows preciously near

Dear Mr Facebook.

Dear Mr Facebook, would you please stop removing my posts

You're standing there watching me write, like some holy ghost

Free speech isn't banned, we're allowed to have our wee digs

Can we not speak of men, I assume, who're romancing dead pigs?

Can I not criticise a government who show me contempt

Or these huge corporations who think, from tax, they're exempt?

Can I not vent my anger when you start breaching my human rights?

Like you've done to some of my friends, and me just last night!

But maybe I should be happy and proud, even dancing with glee

That of all of the people on Facebook world, you happily chose little me.

Big Brown Envelopes.

I heard a tall tale, from a taxman who'd failed

He mentioned a store they call Boots

He then whispered some words, that were just so absurd

He said that more of them are in cahoots

He then got quite abrupt and said this government's corrupt

And Boots don't pay tax on their drugs

I said look in my eyes, do I look surprised

They do nothing but take us for mugs.

Mr Starspangled Starbucks, who don't give a fcuk

Think they're the Crème de la Crème

People buy one caffe and sit there all day

The Mafia's got nothing on them

Well, Ebay's another, you can auction your mother

But who d'you think's in on the act

But if a loophole's undone, you can blame only one

The man at the top – that's a fact.

You know Amazon's cheap and says it's here for keeps

And they'll tell us they love Britain's shores

They're not here for the view, they want me and you

We're just corporate tax bloody whores.

This Great British kindness, is not financial blindness

Look away if you don't want to see more

No, they're not so blind, they're rewarded in kind

With a brown envelope through their door.

They talk of corruption, of social disruption

You'd think we were governed by gents

But they're so bloody lax, on those Corporates' tax

And blame the poor for 1.7%

It's always the poor, not the rich or grandeur

They swear to their god made of gold

And as you live out your time, they'll live on in crime

You're still tied to them when you are old.

The City of Souls.

They sleep in the doorways of dark lanes and alleys

Away from the bright city lights

They don't make a fuss as they shelter from us,

Ashamed, they stay out of sight.

But what of their future and what of their past,

Do we shun them because of their crimes?

But we look into their heads and find out instead

They're just us who've hit on hard times.

Another night in the city

Behind the bright lights

Lie those we refuse to console

Well you just failed the test

If you thought you'd progressed

Here in the city of souls.

They're here in their thousands and beg cap in hand

Some say they're the scourge of our streets

And those who decry them walk past and deny them

And point to their cup of deceit.

Their wind blows so cold, it goes right to their soul

And their breath freezes in the night air

It's a life they don't choose and they've no more to lose

Where the danger of sleep brings despair.

They've committed no crime but they're still serving time

The "unfortunates" some don't want to know

Born and bred in this land, life's now out of their hands

They are home but there's nowhere to go

They're not refugees, they're ours on their knees

With failings and frailties and faults

All our housing demands are for others' commands

But our cash finds its way to their vaults.

We're too quick to disown those we call our own

And include some we used to call friends

They're down on their luck and some don't give a fuck

And that's not how this story should end,

Even vets live in fear and it takes volunteers

To build homes to house all our brave

A quick refurb is great but for some it's too late

They've already found peace in their graves.

Farcical.

They're The Brothers elite and they're not so discreet

They're just people whose lives are a farce

For in life's golden lottery only fools contract snobbery

As they pick another rose from their arse

That deep penetration, gives them such elation,

As they trip over egos so big

They damn all without and leave us in no doubt

That when they punch, we feel their digs

Their aloofness is blest by some snobbish club crest

Endorsed by their wannabe peers

But they know how to hurt and they treat us like dirt

Even their silence can damage our ears.

They think it so funny when they tear up their money

Then shite in some Bullingdon sink

But with their snobbish noses, all they smell are roses

They think that their shite doesn't stink

And think they're so pretty with farts like confetti

Rose petals fly out of their arse

They're The Brothers elite and they're not so discreet

They're just people whose lives are a farce.

We're Here!

Some say we're pure mental for standing so idly by

Don't confuse words like mental with stupid, we're still saying Aye!

They're trying their best to destroy us by warping our minds

And those who don't want to know are towing their line.

When you've nothing to fight with, the only hope you have is fear

They're still running on empty and their leader's now been made a peer

Well Darling we marched in your city but you weren't there

And the next day thousands marched, danced and sang in Glasgow's George Square.

The next stop is Dundee and that'll be jumping and packed out as well

You still don't know why we rally or the story we tell

We have risen and rising and that should tell you we're not going away

We don't care what you broadcast or print or what Westminster says.

We unfurled their flag that was held together with lies

But when we hit back we are told, we can't criticise

We're still waiting on answers from questions, even now we're still being denied

And we know they don't have the answers so they run back to London to hide.

They sit on the edge of a throne that's on temporary lease

Then progress as lords to a house where most are deceased

Where, by signing a book they can sleep or just sign on and go

Our plight is not their concern, they don't want to know.

Westminster knows Scotland is rising and ignoring their fear

To them, it's the edge of the world, it's the final frontier

We are deeply divided yet they pretend that nothing is wrong

The rich just get richer and the poor are put where they belong.

We are not opportunists but a representation of all

Who despise their manoeuvres, their deceit, their lies and their gall

We come from all creeds, every race yet they won't hear our voice

But the destruction of parties in Scotland shows we have a choice.

Twa Dugs.

She yelped and she yelped then crawled to his side

Her love and affection she could no longer hide

She bows down to no-one or so it would appear

The Dug fae The Dale just snarls and sneers.

She obeys all her masters no matter their stance

And stares open eyed as though lost in a trance

Another master has spoken and their thoughts don't align

So just like before she changes her mind!

Panting and puffing with weird howling wails

You can't help but feel sorry for The Dug fae The Dale

And again she will stop and with that trademark long stare

She's searching for something but that something's not there.

Is it guidance she seeks or some help from above

Or maybe she's lonely and looking for love.

Do those long vacant gazes reflect what's in her brain

She keeps us amused but she drives us insane

But The Dug fae The Dale's like a mad dog on heat

And it's The Wee Ginger Dug that she's dying to meet.

Corbyn and Scotland.

You looked so important in front of your crowd

But your voice was so silent when it once was so loud

There was no mention of Trident, it wasn't even discussed

And your stance on the poor left us all in disgust.

Two weeks in the job and they've brought you to heel

You betrayed your own principles; tell me how does that feel?

Your snipes at the Nationalists, the Scots own SNP

If you're insulting them then you're insulting me

With your misinformation but I prefer to say lies,

Is the cause of your party's catastrophic demise.

The failures, the heartaches, they're all faults you've disowned

And when you go to your bed you should sleep on your own,

You just don't get Scotland, its people, their aim

But to you, we're the problem, the source of your blame.

Edinburgh South's your Republic, that's all you control

Your other forty right wingers are still claiming the dole,

We left you in tears and you're still drying your eyes

And your one solitary MP is a feat you disguise.

It seems you learned nothing as you're still riling Scots

You ignored all our warnings, you're still Westminster taught

Even now you back Osborn and his austere regime

Oh! You and The Dug will make some bloody team!

You cry Scotland Come Home, come back to the fold

Well, the sheep here are deaf and don't do as they're told

We've heard all your rhetoric, your insults and lies

But you still haven't listened and won't be criticised

I thought you were noble but you're just as deranged

You haven't changed Labour, it's you, Labour has changed!

You've answers to nothing but still promise the earth

But the betrayal of yourself, showed us exactly your worth.

Work, Rest and Play.

Some praise nuclear warheads which will never be used

Deterrents we call them, are our brains being abused?

Uncle Sam says we need them; there may be threats from the east

And that it just takes one nutter and we'll all be deceased.

That's rich from a nation, who's at war every day

To them that's just normal, it's their work, rest and play

Yet it's China we've gone to who last week were the threat,

Well, they'll build nuclear plants here and we're told not to fret!

Are they our new allies? Is there something I've missed?

What's happening here, I just don't get the gist!

They'll be built by the Chinese with help from the French

It gets more confusing as the lies leave their stench.

Some questions were answered and accepted by all

It's cheered by Westminster when they should be appalled

Can somebody help me, someone in the know

Whose side are we on now, who's running this show?

Hand to Mouth.

Oh! The brains of those who rule

Are seen by most as bloody fools

They say that war will bring us peace

But some who fought are now deceased

They feed the rich, not food, but wealth

And from the poor they take their health

The few who've most rule this land

And the "hand to mouth", they cannot stand.

Your Castle on a Hill.

Ye perch yersels on Calton Hill

Or a hill by any name

And play yer fiddles tae the tune

Whilst ignoring a' the flames

Kings and Queens some think ye are

In yer castles in the sky

And do nothing as yer country burns,

Oor cultures fade an' die.

Ye watched the crofters sail away

And those who stayed lay dead

Burnt alive within their homes

Or when rafters crushed their heads.

Oor ancient tongue sae colourful

Was cut oot by the sword

And aye, we stood and watched the foe

That bastard Scottish Lord

And like the sheep that roamed the land

Being fattened for the kill

We stand and watch those deaths again

From oor castle on a hills.

Like then oor tongues are silent

As though the past has been restored

Some will speak whilst others won't

They still fear their overlords.

The Fab Four fae Orkney.

Once again they've gone silent on the Carmichael case,

Now the Fab Four fae Orkney, could be winning the race,

They've amassed a great fortune to fight alleged crimes

Yet the arm of our government won't give it their time.

They're taking our money but don't take our views

BBC is still biased, it's been dropped from their news.

There's a court case impending but you'd never have guessed

Carmichael's a huge case but it's not been addressed

But they'll rant about Thomson which I think is right

While the Fab Four fae Orkney continue their fight.

On the Forth Road Bridge were thousands saying Don't Drill Our lands

Protesters, from all walks, in peace, holding hands

Not a murmur was heard on BBC's local news

They just do as they're told and reject Scottish views.

They're liars and bigots, they're biased, they're done

They're the arm of the government and their corporate sons.

They ignore the real news and the deaths on their streets

And still bow to your Mafia, Westminster's elite

But the Fab Four fae Orkney have the backing of stars

Whilst Carmichael festers in some Westminster bars

As he sips favoured whiskies and swigs of his ales

Then praying to god they don't sling him in jail.

Has he ready his answers for the questions they'll ask

For that seat in the dock is not for him to just bask

He's abused his constituents, his position and power

It's the Fab Four fae Orkney v the Westminster shower?

Their Plastic Thrones.

They sit on their moral high ground, the pinnacle of their breed

And hide behind the monuments built to those who have decreed

That poverty's a necessity, caused by the richest of our age

And most take in all their fancy words then rise up with their rage.

They condemn the poor, the pensioners, those arriving on our shores

They'll shove the blame on anyone deflecting what they've got in store

They're the dregs of our society, whose fantasies are real

Realising all their dreams as they plunder, loot and steal

Whilst behind the scenes, their media, assist with all that's wrong

And in frenzied panic show us they've been hand in hand too long.

Neither speak up for the people but assume opinions for us all

And take pleasure in the lies they tell then watch us fight and brawl

Their aim; divide and conquer as our in-house fights progress

We can't move on, we can't unite, their lies leave us distressed

We unfriend, attack, we criticise, when once we were as one

And everything we've built up, they have expertly undone

Their callousness is their trademark with an arrogance never seen

Not even back in Thatcher's reign when we raged on her machine

But this party of the people have shown they're anything but

By showering us with ridicule then enforcing all their cuts

Have they lived in our high rise flats, were they born in single ends

Yet know what's always right for us and address us all as friends

Do friends of yours encourage death or insist that you don't eat

Or threaten hypothermia by denying you of heat,

This insistence is an evil pact which they impose upon the poor

And grin as you lay dying in their created stench and stoor.

A sect so rich in poverty that they seek our full demise

For riches from the poorest lives are what sparkle in their eyes.

Their endorsements are divisional, delusional and say that we're neurotic

Yet they indulge in all this sufferance and proclaim they're patriotic.

They're calculated psychopaths with a doctrine all their own

And accept the poor are ignorant and are standing all alone

But they cannot see or understand their time is at an end

But the rise of all our countries have shown their kind have no friends.

They're slipping down their pedestals and sliding off their seats

And still they cannot see the rise that will bring on their defeat.

Premier Pork.

This isn't George Orwell and his Animal Farm

But an alleged story of Dave and his intimate charms,

He sighed then he wept for it was too late to save

The girl of his dreams; she'd been sent to her grave.

There's a rumour they all went for a drink down the pub

Where they initiated plans for a secret wee club

They shouted Hurrah! As they ran out the door

Then burned all their money in front of the poor.

This life without love would fill him with dread

So, as a gift from his friends, they cut off her head

And laid out on her salver he could see in her eyes

That love was still there despite her demise.

The Dave fella embraced her blushing pink snout

Yet none of his friends were surprised or freaked out

But assumed that their friend had gone out of his head

Not because of a pig: But because it was dead!

The Great Chinese Takeaway.

Repossessions, evictions, all over the town

Offices empty and shops all closed down

Boarded up windows where a sign says To Let

Life under The Tories only builds up your debts!

They're crippling our workforce, no jobs to be found

And from the steelworks of Britain, we hear not a sound

Their voice is not heard, their tears are not seen

As China sits feasting in the house of the queen.

China's renowned for their sub-standard steel

Worldwide structures buckle, so what's the appeal

New Zealand and others have learned from mistakes

It seems Britain is playing for the highest of stakes!

There's no other country who would sell out their own

And be controlled by a country, their own citizens disown

Is our security threatened by their dubious past?

Will their nuclear reactor be just one massive blast?

China travelled through Whitehall in a carriage of gold

A right royal ride for the rich to behold

But as they feast on their banquets in the bright city lights

Will there be mention of their famed human Rights?

We've seen plants destroyed and our funding withdrawn

As this most evil of parties are the devil's own spawn

They'll bastardise all leaving us high and dry

This "party for workers" are still living their lie.

Do they not realise the cruel damage they've done

Can they not feel the tears of their of their countries' own sons

Do they fear for a future? I don't think they can

They're out to destroy every woman and man.

We Are.

The all-consuming winds of change have blown through our years

That energy still haunts us now but now we shrug those fears

Our troubled spirits never rest even when death takes its toll

We are the muck, we are the dirt, we are the Scottish soul.

We are the very monuments upon whose land we thrive

Our commitment takes us on the path where true hearts feel alive

Where its softness blends with bitter edge, so compelling to the eyes

Yet where convention dare not live, below or on the skies.

We identify this constant change that pours our rugged land,

This portrays who and what we are, each woman, child and man.

We immerse in Scotland's wilderness and drawn to stories from our past

But our own life is our history and that history's unsurpassed.

We sculpt out souls which we adapt in a landscape nature gave

Then call upon our ancestors from beyond their hallowed graves

To discover they are really us, we are the past that's come again

We are the skies, we are the land, we are the people, sovereign.

The Crawling Mind.

With no consent or pleasantries, the beasts prey on my mind

And who knows what they look for or what they hope to find

You delve into, with piercing eyes, my deepest, darkest thoughts,

And tell me you've unraveled this mind of tangled knots.

I know you're all around me with your technicolour eye

And like all the great detectives, you're the mist of passers-by

But you're in the air, the air I breathe, yet you're not here at all

Yes, you are invisible but through my mind I feel you crawl.

You sit with me when going to work yet no-one's next to me

You watch me read and write or call but no-one's there to see

You follow me around my day, carrying out my tasks

And never question what I do and have no need to ask.

You know me and who I am and know I disapprove

And yet you get beneath my skin, forecasting my next move

Yes, you shadow me around like some prying evil ghost

So should I feel an honour here, enough for me to boast?

Who are you or what are you? The clock keeps ticking on

And though I'm helpless in my sleep, you watch me until dawn

You hear the words I do not speak and think you read my thoughts

Am I unruly or a threat? Have you thought, I may be not?

The School of Fools.

These people fly in graceless flight revered by witless fools

Let them be ruled by flushing lords from yonder stately schools

Finery is defined by mind and not by class or garb

For these lords will stab you in the back, their lies have steely barbs.

Let my eyes go up the path and gaze my dreamy glen

And let them fleet through bracken braes

Where waters fall from granite rocks, clear and cool and sweet

And rest upon the greenest grass where lads and lassies meet

An idle cave where lovers go where hearts can be alone

They're riches of the human kind, not monuments of stone.

Carry me so far away from lives that know not life

Take me from the daily spew of greed, distress and strife

Where walkers are just cast aside, now everyone must run

Where lives are mapped and buried before that life's begun.

They race from cradle to the grave not knowing life exists

They have not felt the summer dew or autumn's rolling mists

The leafy suburbs, their domain, like pastoral lives before

They tread the quaint stockbroker's belts like their thieving lords before

On and on and on it goes but this thieving has to end

And I, for one, will keep them out, I am not these people's friend.

All Under One Banner.

None are so fervent or rich in their thoughts

They share every hope, every dream

Their sole aim in life's to unite every Scot

But nothing is easy it seems

All Under One Banner, they'll step out today

And march with their heads held up high

They speak with one voice, they now have no choice

Saying Scots' Independence is nigh.

Their neighbours they'll meet as they march down the streets

Of the city that goes round and round

There's been recent upheaval and that's all down to Evel

The Tories have proven they're clowns

Westminster's brass have stamped us second class

And endorsed this change is for good

But the mood of this country has changed

They think they have style but this is just vile

It looks like Westminster's estranged.

They marched to the pipes, and the boron beat loud

And came to rest in Glasgow Green

They were honoured by guards, our roadways own bards

The Yes bikers revved up their machines.

They rode to the cause to oppose Evel laws

As the marchers beside them now stood

Side by side, hand in hand, they showed love for their land

Are you listening now Holyrood?

The Cauldron.

It wasn't us who chose this path

But we've now to listen to them laugh

They're pointing in our naïve direction

But outside they stand they're almost bare

The children with the helpless stare

These young ones of our future need protection.

These chosen men and women play,

They leave our hearts in disarray

Slaying every sister and her brother

The gamblers squeal with oddest ease

But the cauldron keeps us on our knees

And the only care they know is for each other.

They bluff their way with ice cold eyes

And play the card from where it lies

The one-eyed Jacks play their game of poker

They decide which hand is shown

And they decide which hand is thrown

We are their bluff and they, they are the jokers.

The King, The Queen, The lowly Knave

Stand laughing at the undug graves

They're judge and jury, they're the hangman's noose

The cauldron breeds this man of gold

Who, for a penny, buys a poor man's soul

Deciding let him hang or turn him loose.

And the benches where they spend their days

Remind them of the smooth green baize

And the cards, face up, reveal how many die

They fake the tears for soldiers, dead

Then dream the next war in their head

As the poppy that they're wearing starts to cry.

As the gamblers keep their bloody score

The cauldron always asks for more

But the gamblers here are only here on lease

They don't think of those who fought and fell

The men and women forced through hell

But most of all they never think of peace.

Soon the cards begin to fold

The people see through men of gold

And the rag doll lies beside the girl who cries

Now the bankers play the gamblers' role

Foretelling what our futures hold

By creating, the world we love's, demise.

How many wars before it's the last

Have we learned nothing from the past

As the cauldron fuels hatred for a fight

Gone are the days of volunteers

Press ganged into death with peers

Have the people of our countries seen the light?

The odds they give will pay, they say

But the betting slip is just one way

We'll be dead before the race is over

For the gamblers are the bankers here

The cauldron is their house of fear

Until we stand the truth won't be uncovered.

A Dreamer's Dream.

They rule us with impunity, in every town, community

All they do is try to put us down

If fighting's what it's all about, they'll get their fight, I have no doubt

The bell is ringing for the second round.

It's a place where hearts and minds collide but when you feed in people's pride

Confusion turns to trust within a nation

If freedom's just a dream away then don't let this dream hide

Westminster's words were never our salvation.

You think you stand and speak for all but soon you'll see your towers fall

This country was never meant for you

This kingdom is now torn apart; we'll liberate and free their hearts

This nation has a different point of view.

We've a wrongly titled reigning queen and a history that's so obscene

From manufactured stories full of lies

Tell me, who and what are we, we'll find those truths when we are free

And no longer will we be sacrificed.

Our laws are made by those deranged, the strangers laws will all be changed

This nation will have its independence

We'll celebrate a nation's choice and across this land we will rejoice

And you my friend will not be in attendance.

Things were bad but now they're worse and what's to come is one more curse

A curse on you and all your richly gains

And one last word before I leave, that very soon you all will grieve

No more will we be tethered to your chains.

We'll have the key of liberty and set this nation's people free

A country where its natives pass the laws

Where its people make the rules and not a country run by Eton's fools

We'll even put that in a special clause.

You quote the lord and his good book but tell me when did you last look

At the double standards of your friends' behaviour

Some knew the facts but would not tell, I hope your lord sends them to hell!

Freedom from you all will be our saviour.

Don't Bomb Syria.

She looks around her bombed out shell

And cries from where her parents fell

Her mother, father, blown away

You knew them not but made them pay

And blood streams from eyes that cannot see

As she feels her way on hands and knees

Through blood soaked stones where she once lived

Which god will she, at three, forgive?

Her neighbours run, scream as they flee

Yes Westminster; Refugees!

They run from bombs that you sent here

While you tell civilians; Do not fear

But no-one hears the little girl

They too are helpless in their world

Their world collapsed because of you

What are your plans when war is through?

She looks for help but cannot see

Which country takes blind refugees?

She's orphaned by those bombs you sent

And blinded by the hate you vent

And you fuel hatred on these shores

So you can have your terror wars

You say extremists Muslims are to blame

But Muslims state: Not In My Name!

While in Syria you employ your fate

You kill them then ask us, donate

And you tell us they're in desperate need

But these children died because of greed

Your greed, not ours, yours alone

These wars you want, we all condone

You bomb Africa, the middle east

When all the people want is peace.

Her brother lies down by her side

But she doesn't know that he has died

She's all alone with no-one near

And yes she feels Westminster's fear

At three she sits, and red tears, cries

And she'll sit and cry until she dies

Outside her home that's now a shell

The one Westminster turned into her hell.

Here's Yer Hogmanay!

Their champagne is our cup of tea, their canapés our bread

They laugh and scoff at all of us but it's us who made their bed

Their caviar in silver pots, our toast served on a plate

Aye! Rightly they can scorn us for it's us who sealed our fate.

They can line their corporate pockets as the hungry lie in bed

We gave them all this power, we gave them the go-ahead

And while they run their biased BBC and their media nationwide

They can bolster windows, doors and gates but they can never hide

For their past will come to haunt them like the reaper's deathly ghost

And when it does, we'll all be there, and this will be our toast:

Nae mair will we bow down tae ye

Nae mair we'll be yer slaves

There'll come a day when we'll be free

E'en those you put in graves

And the ghosts of a' that you have wranged

Are waiting for this day

Aye! The ghosts of a' who've lain lang

Will hae their liberty!

So here's tae us on Hogmanay

And tae every absent friend

Raise yer glass tae yin an' a'

This is no' the end.

My Opinion.

In this democratic country I am entitled, as everyone else is, to vote for the person and Party I think best for me.

So don't come here to my door with your Conservative or Labour Party Propaganda pamphlets telling me your politics are better than those of anti-austerity from The Nazis of The North or the deluded Green Party. Your democracy doesn't work. The greatest rise in any business is that of foodbanks which is disgusting considering the richest have doubled their wealth in the past ten years while these free foodbanks, paid for by the people and not our politicians, have increased by 1600% over the past 5 years.

You can tell me all you want and it's not that I won't listen, it's just that I am fed up listening to all your lies based on the bungs you get via big brown envelopes or extra shares in some vast arms company, who then twist your arm to go into other's countries and bomb them so your dividends will rise, whilst ignoring the starving around you. The biggest threat to the British people is the corrupt British government itself.

Many people said it'll never change but is that because people are afraid of change or have no faith in any politician? Is that because they paid out bankers their highest ever bonuses last year whilst claiming £89bn on expenses for themselves? I'm not saying the SNP are angels but their expenses are a fraction of the main parties per head with Alex Salmond giving away to charity half of his annual salary.

Something has to change and the people of Scotland should not be afraid of change, they are fighting for a government that will stand for all the people against the elitists that rule us just now. Neither are they anti-English as the media suggests, in fact not only suggest but instigate. The first six people I met in Glasgow's Hope Over Fear rally last Saturday were English, from Cambridge and York. BBC reported 100 people attended whilst Police Scotland and STV reported 12,000. They also tell you that

Nicola Sturgeon wants another referendum. Nicola Sturgeon has never said this and has no authority of when and if there will be another, that is down to the people of Scotland. This vote is for a General Election in which we all have to work together and the electorate will choose their MP, wherever they are in the UK through a democratic voting system.

Listening to the government owned media will not tell you the truth; you will only hear what they want you to hear! Make your own informed choice but do some back ground work first.

Twenty minutes after writing this a guy from the Labour Party knocked at the door stating that they never overspent in their last term in office and that Gordon Brown is a great Scottish Socialist! He also said I have two choices and that the Greens couldn't do anything nor did Miliband say he would not do a deal with SNP. I asked him in to listen to the recordings of him saying it, he refused. Door shut! My raised voice seemed to upset the candidate, Ruth Cadbury, as she rushed passed the house while the woman across the road scurried away into her car. SNP sticker outside now in west London.

Do We Matter?

It should have been so much better. For everyone! People always say: you'll never change it OR them, that's the system, the way it works.

Scotland did!

They were lost in a society like everyone else, where nothing changed as they'd hoped, walking about in a mist and being told what to do by the ruling class of Westminster. A neighbour in London on Thursday said, we are controlled by Eton. A fair point considering our rulers were educated there or of that ilk. He went onto say they were shafted there (Scotland) and now taking their revenge by shafting us. Again, another fair point.

Do we really matter, any of us? Do governments work for the people? The simple answer is No. They work for conglomerates, corporations and of course are told what to say by their rulers, The Banks.

The government and their media swerve the questions asked by avoiding them. But they always do that and we let them away with it? But why?! They avoid and are let off because they have asked these questions to themselves and don't like what they hear and the good old media forgive them and let them ramble. As they've always done.

What happened is Scotland was seismic. That northern wind of change swept through all of Scotland then stops very suddenly at the borders and below that line, the real desolation begins – all the way down to London where a temperate climate always exists. No-one anywhere could say that the last five years have been beneficial to the people but to vote for more of it is exactly what's been done. £12bn in cuts to come but no-one can answer where the cuts are coming from and they still get into power. No answer but more to the point, no-one pushed for an any answers. A ten second push and then the laugh and move onto the next question. This only cements our governments have taken over the mind of our reporters in their ownership of the media.

The SNP never took away Labour's votes or stole their seats, the UK as a whole done that. Labour failed dramatically in Scotland and fared not much better in England and Wales. Why? They had no social policies worthy of a "X" in that wee box. The Tories had nothing either but they stoked the fire of nationalism with threats that Labour would do a coalition with the nasty Nazis from Jockistan then just sat back and watched Labour crumble. The very thought of Scotland having any say in this democratic Union sent tremors through the Tory benches so played up the English nationalist card. Almost daily the media spoke about the hatred coming from Scotland towards the English and how, if SNP aligned with Labour, they could destroy the Union. Labour were forced to retort with a promise they would not form a coalition with the SNP at any cost.

This not only helped kill Labour off in Scotland but showed the Tories their plan was working. They then sat back and watched Labour capitulate. Hate from this government showed through towards the Scots and knew it would harm Labour in Scotland. Again Scottish votes did not matter as the government they never chose, got in.

David Cameron laughed off the racist remarks from Boris Johnson against the Scots and refused to act on it by saying, that's Boris' way, he's a colourful character but if Ukip candidates had said it: they would have seen a yellow card at least. The seeds grew and the growth of propaganda continued. This was never about Scotland v England or whoever, this election was about fairness. The rich double their wealth as the foodbanks rise by a massive 1600% to help the poor working families of this unequal Union, this already divided UK. These foodbanks are not just in Scotland. There are some in London but go outside London and you will see them.

This Tory government have been given a free hand to rule with an iron rod. This party never got in through its exemplary policies but by the lack of choice in policies from any other UK party. The Scots saw through the lies and deceit and decided to do something about it. They had had enough and voted SNP. They wanted change and voted for it with their main aim to end austerity through the UK. Now, we all have to wait. The SNP face a massive task but it is all down to Mr Cameron and if he wants to play ball.

The thought of an Independence Referendum was never on the agenda from the SNP and was never mentioned by them but it was brought up daily, as much as twenty times a day by the main UK political parties. You just had to switch on the news or pick up a paper and there it was. Divide and conquer yet again. Even up until the last day, it was being asked. Are our media that much in the back pocket of governments that they cannot understand even the most simplistic of answers? Of that, I am certain.

This was another nail in Labour's massive coffin and supplied freely by all and sundry and one which the English voter fell for. Labour lost this election in England as the voters chose Conservative on the day and in doing so voted for that £12bn cuts in welfare aimed at the poor. This Union of equals is riddled with inequality throughout its lands. Scots recognised this but it seems the rest of the UK are happy to be subservient and go along with becoming poorer each year. Or were they that afraid of a coalition between Labour and the SNP. Sit back and watch the rich get richer whilst our poor get poorer or even die. I'm alright Jack.

The parties failed, yes. So did the people of the rest of the UK for not doing something about it. Scots weren't happy with Labour and done something about it. The rest in general showed apathy and believed the hype and hatred of the Tories instead of doing something about it. They work for you, not vice versa. Hold them to account. Or just wait as we've always done, do nothing and hope.

I was ecstatic when the SNP got in, it gave Westminster the shake-up it so badly needed and I seriously thought that the rest of the UK wanted rid of austerity but I was so very wrong. But this is a democracy we live in where everyone has their opinion and we must stick by that. However, I think apathy played a huge part. The truth is out there but too many of us refuse to believe it and think it just lies or conspiracy theories because it is not reported on the mainstream media.

I thank each and every single one of you for giving me that wake-up call and encouraging and supporting me in the past three years. I am now awake thanks to you. One day Scotland will be independent and the whole truth will come out.

Thank you to everyone who supported me throughout this project. That's just about everyone from The Yes Campaign because without your support and encouragement, this book would not have been possible. Thank you once again. Paul x

Printed in Great Britain
by Amazon

33665361R00145